A Cloud of Witnesses

...great theological insights for today's Church

Joe M. Thomas, Ph.D.

WIPF & STOCK · Eugene, Oregon

Wipf and Stock Publishers
199 W 8th Ave, Suite 3
Eugene, OR 97401

A Cloud of Witnesses
. . . Great Theological Insights for Today's Church
By Thomas, Joe M.
Copyright©2014 by Thomas, Joe M.
ISBN 13: 978-1-5326-9321-2
Publication date 6/4/2019
Previously published by Ekklesia, 2014

This book is dedicated to

My Family

TABLE OF CONTENTS

FOREWORD	vi
PREFACE	vii
ACKNOWLEDGMENTS	ix

CHAPTER ONE - St. Augustine
*Original Sin and the Distinction Between
the Good of Marriage and the Corruption of Human Nature* — 11

CHAPTER TWO - Roberto de Nobili
Christ and Culture in the Theological Method — 33

CHAPTER THREE - Herman Dooyeweerd
Sphere Sovereignty and Modality: A Conceptual Introduction — 51

CHAPTER FOUR - Karl Rahner
Original Sin in the Light of the Human Situation — 63

CHAPTER FIVE - Karl Barth
The Meaning of the Baptism of the Holy Spirit — 71

CHAPTER SIX - Karl Barth
A Theology of Human Work — 89

CHAPTER SEVEN - Bernard Lonergan
The Notion of Communications in the Theological Method — 104

CHAPTER EIGHT - J. Severino Croatto
The Use of the Exodus Motif in the Liberation Hermeneutics — 118

CHAPTER NINE - Lesslie Newbigin
The Concept of 'Religion' and Salvation of Non-Christians — 139

FOREWORD

Dr. Joe Thomas has asked me to write a few words about his present volume. As a colleague and friend, I am delighted to comply with his request. Dr. Thomas has been quite successful in bringing out invaluable insights from the history of Christian theology to bear upon the contemporary mission of the Church. Each chapter in the book ends with some practical suggestions to inform our Christian ministry. Such insights come from the crosscultural experiences of the author.

Any present theological investigation has to take into account what great theologians of the past have accomplished for us. Professor Thomas has selected the works of some great theologians of the church for his project. This book is an attempt to inform the Christian mind about the need for ongoing conversation between the past and the present in doing theology in a modern cultural context.

This work demonstrates the author's commitment to preserve the modern Church's theological heritage by engaging, interpreting, and communicating the works of great luminaries of the past.

Professor Gary Staats, Th.D., Ph.D., D.S. Litt.
Gale & Harriette Ritz Professor of Old Testament
Winebrenner Theological Seminary

PREFACE

Gordon Haddon Clark begins his 1984 work *In Defense of Theology* with the following comment: "Theology, once acclaimed 'the Queen of the Sciences,' today hardly rises to the rank of a scullery maid; it is often held in contempt, regarded with suspicion, or just ignored." The status of theology as an academic discipline has declined sharply over the last three decades due to the rapid convergence and synthesis of a number of religious, cultural, and economic factors. The theological seminary as a place of intellectual preparation for future ministers of the church is also in serious crisis. The sustained reflection on the Word of God and its theological expression in the modern Western culture has been suppressed by the factors that I have mentioned above. The typical local church in today's America is marked by biblical illiteracy and doctrinal ignorance. As an intellectual discipline, theology must be given the greatest attention by all Christians, which is essential to preserving the truth of the church. It is this message that I want to communicate through the publication of this book, which is a product of my own study.

Much of the current confusion in the life of the Church stems from a neglect of the Holy Scriptures and the doctrines that they set forth. It is important to state that our personal study of theology will prove surprisingly fruitful and intellectually invigorating. It is my conviction that systematic theology must become a lifelong activity of the Christian mind, without which no meaningful religious life is possible. The teachings of Jesus and his apostles and the theological activities of the early Church are both an example and an inspiration for doing theology in our own day. As the writer of this book, I have benefited from the doctrinal discourses and theological methods of the great theologians, whose works I have engaged in these chapters. It is with this benefit in mind that I offer this work for a wider readership.

This study begins with St. Augustine, whose writings have influenced Western civilization in many ways. The last chapter is on Lesslie Newbigin, whose writings have made a lasting impact on our understanding of the nature of religion. My personal friendship with Bishop Newbigin and the inspiration that I have drawn from him and his writings have been theologically enriching.

The major purpose of publishing this book is to make the exposition of various theological themes readily available to students who have to undertake theology seminars on a regular basis. Furthermore, as St. Paul said, there is a vital link between doctrine and life: "Watch your life and doctrine closely. Persevere in them, because if you do, you will save both yourself and your hearers" (1 Tim. 4:16, NIV).

ACKNOWLEDGEMENTS

The contents of this book are academic papers that I presented at theology seminars in Toronto. The chapters on Roberto De Nobili, Karl Rahner, Bernard Lonergan, and Lesslie Newbigin were published earlier as essays in *Mission Today: A New Journal of Ecumenical and Missiological Research*. They are included with permission. All of them deal with theological method.

The primary purpose of publishing this book is for my students to have access to major voices of the Christian past, which are invaluable for our continuing discussions in theology. By undertaking this effort, I affirm our continuity with these great theologians' contributions. Thus, St. Augustine, De Nobili, Rahner, Newbigin, and all the others mentioned herein continue to speak to us in the Church.

I am grateful for the encouragement of the Rt. Rev. Dr. Bill Atwood, the Bishop of the International Diocese, Anglican Church in North America, without whose help this book would not have been published.

I am thankful to Ekklesia Society Publications for its willingness to publish this monograph. I thank Dr. Lee Ligon-Borden for her invaluable comments and suggestions. In the editing process and overall formatting of the manuscript, I owe much to Lee, who did an excellent work in her role as editor.

I am thankful for the works of the ICS professors in Dooyeweerdian philosophy. Many of these works have been readily available to me from the time of my study and research in Toronto.

Finally, I am thankful to my family, especially my wife Anita, for her love and care, and our children, Susan, Nathan, and Roshan, in whom we see the grace of God at work.

I present this humble work to my colleagues and students with the hope that the readers become familiar with the doctrines expounded herein. I acknowledge the works of all who helped in the publication of this book.

Chapter One

ST. AUGUSTINE

Original Sin and the Distinction Between the Good of Marriage and the Corruption of Human Nature

St. Augustine is (354-430) regarded as one of the greatest theologians and an outstanding Father of the Church. His theology has influenced not only the life of the Church but also the various spheres of Western civilization. The doctrine of original sin is a major subject in the writings of St. Augustine, especially in those books that deal with human nature and marriage. *De Nuptiis et Concupiscentia* sets forth this subject matter clearly. The work has the character of Christian apologetics.[1] In it, St. Augustine makes a clear distinction between the good of human nature as the creation of God and the corruption of human nature due to original sin. He further distinguishes between the good of marriage and the evil of concupiscence that is associated with marriage. The writing on marriage and concupiscence shows a clear distinction between the good work of God and the corrupting work of the devil. These theological writings have played a significant role in the Church's attitude to marriage and sexuality.

The subject of the present study is based on the two treatises of St. Augustine called *De Nuptiis et Concupiscentia*. The particular focus is on Augustine's distinction between the created good of human nature and its subsequent corrupted nature, as well as the distinction between the good of marriage and the evil of lust in a marriage relationship. These two distinctions are discussed in relation to original sin. The major tasks

---

[1] These are written not only to refute the Pelagian misconceptions and misinterpretations of Augustine's words, but also for making the biblical teaching on the topic clear and thereby `bringing aid to Christian faith by defending it' in accordance with the apostolic admonition. The entire work is interwoven with scriptures. References are made especially to 1 Peter 3:15 and Col. 4:6.

of this chapter are to discuss these basic distinctions in relation to the doctrine of original sin and to comment on their implications to the life of the Church.

Three general observations about the treatises are in order at the outset. In the *first* place, Augustine affirms the goodness of marriage against the Manichees in both these two works and *Contra Faust* (6.3). Marriage is good because it was instituted and blessed by God, its status subsequently was raised to that of Christ's union with the Church, and present within it are three virtuous aspects, namely, *proles, fides,* and *sacramentum*. In the *second* place, the treatises contain a Creation-Fall-Redemption structure that underlies the entire discussion of the theme. *Finally*, the doctrine of Regeneration is a strong motif in Augustine's theological vision of marriage and procreation. This is a salvation *motif* that is to be understood in the Trinitarian framework of his thesis.

Polemical Background of Augustine's Work

Augustine's first book, *On Marriage and Concupiscence*, was written in 419 A.D. and found its way into the hands of Julianus (Julian of Eclanum, 380-455), who wrote four books (*Ad Turbantium*) opposing Augustine's views. Excerpts of Julian's work were sent to Count Valerius, who had a "warm and earnest interest in the testimony of the Word of God against the heretics," and directed them to Saint Augustine. Apparently, Julianus twisted Augustine's words, saying that he condemned marriage by maintaining original sin, and this misrepresentation occasioned Augustine's writing of the second book in 420 A.D.

The purpose of his work, as Augustine himself states, is to "distinguish between the evil of carnal concupiscence from which a human is born and therefrom contracts original sin, and the good of marriage."[2] The second treatise is a more pointed attack on the excerpts of Julian's books, because Julian vigorously opposed Augustine's second book by drawing up eight books (*Ad Florum*). As was the case with his several other works, Augustine's two treatises were also developed in the context of the Pelagian controversy.

Julian of Eclanum, one of the most formidable of the Pelagian theologians, had excellent knowledge of Latin, Greek, and Logic and fine secular and theological training. He joined the clergy of his native diocese and later succeeded his father as bishop in 417A.D. He became a strong supporter of Pelagius and in 418 attacked the *Epistola tractoria* of Pope

---

[2] *De Nuptiis*, Book I. I.

Zosimus, in which Pelagius and Coelestius were condemned. He was deposed and expelled from Italy, and his attempts at reconciliation with the Church were unsuccessful. Julian was an able exegete, and his defense of Pelagianism is extant, mainly in citations found in the writings of his opponent, St. Augustine. He accused Augustine of teaching residual Manichaeism or puritanism and opposed the notion of original sin, its consequences, and its transmission through procreation. The Manichaeans maintained that there could be no such thing as innocent sexuality. All sexual activity, in whatever circumstances, aided the powers of the Kingdom of Darkness.[3]

Generally speaking, Julian's teaching on grace can be said to be reductionist in the sense that he reduced it to a simple, protective divine assistance, or a modality extrinsic to the soul. Furthermore, he practically denies the solidarity of the human race in Adam's sin. Julian certainly argues that marriage, conjugal union, and offspring are good, but he differs theologically from Augustine on several points. According to Julian, Augustine holds that concupiscence is evil only in excess.[4] Augustine wrote four tracts against Julian, the last of which was incomplete at his death.

Furthermore, the Pelagian system of teaching, of which Julian was a defender, had many doctrinal errors.[5] The dogmatic errors of Coelestius, an impressive Pelagian theologian, were clearly defined at the Council of Carthage in 411 A.D. *First*, he states that Adam was created mortal and had to die whether or not he sinned. This notion is a negation of the state of original righteousness in which the first man was made. *Second*, the sin of Adam injured himself alone, not the human race. This position is a negation of what is understood as original sin, which passes to subsequent generations. *Third*, infants today are born in the state in which Adam was before his fall. Death and concupiscence are not the results of sin, but the original condition of humanity. *Fourth*, Adam by his death or by his sin did not subject the whole human race to death. This notion is deduced from the fact that Christ by his resurrection does not give life to

---

[3] Peter Brown, *The Body and Society* (New York: Columbia University Press, 1988), 391-92.
[4] J. Bentivegna, "Julian of Eclanum," *New Catholic Encyclopedia*, Vol. 8, William J. McDonald, ed (Washington: The Catholic University of America, 1966), 48.
[5] As a movement, Pelagianism was "multifaceted" and had its own "internal differences." For a succinct treatment of the doctrinal nature of Pelagianism, see Joanne McWilliam, "Pelagius, Pelagianism," *Encyclopedia of Early Christianity*, Everett Ferguson, ed (New York & London: Garland Publishing, 1990), 704.

the entire human race.⁶ When there is a negation of original sin, as Portalie indicates, there is also a negation of the supernatural elevation of the first man before the fall. ⁷ Another question that arises from Pelagianism is the fate of infants who die without baptism. They enjoy eternal life in consequence of the lack of original sin, but they nonetheless are considered excluded from the Kingdom of heaven. But how this is different from the state of eternal life is a question that needs to be answered.⁸

Augustine's treatises on marriage and concupiscence address the issues of original sin, human nature, and baptism of infants in a manner that adequately responds to the questions raised by its polemical context. In both of his treatises, he sees the need for infant baptism as a means by which infants are delivered from the power of darkness. The sacrament of baptism is efficacious in the bestowal of the grace of Christ. By virtue of being born in sin, infants are in the power of the devil, and they renounce this power by the hearts and mouths of those who bring them to baptism.⁹

The Distinction Between the Good of Human Nature and Its Corruption

The two books on marriage and concupiscence draw a clear distinction between the goodness of human nature through divine creation and the corruption of human nature through original sin. If God is the author of the former, the devil is the author of the latter. The corruption of human nature is the consequence of original sin.¹⁰

Augustine's argument is based on the goodness of God, who makes all things good. God is the *summum bonum*, the highest good. Because God is good in himself, He is also good for his creatures. His bountiful dealings with all creatures are manifested in the way in which He extends mercy and care to all, both good and evil. He makes the sun to rise on the evil

---

[6] Eugene Portalie, *A Guide to the Thought of Saint Augustine*, trans. Ralph J. Bastian (London: Burns & Oates, 1960), 184.
[7] Ibid.
[8] Ibid., 185.
[9] *De Nuptiis*, Bk. I, 22.
[10] Later, Augustine makes a further distinction between original sin and actual sins, sins that are "added in every individual man by the motion of his own will." See Bk. II, 46.

and the good, and sends rain on the just and the unjust.[11] His mercy and care are a kindly help, a help to the good nature that He in his goodness has created. Insofar as the human nature is concerned, it is good because of who made it and how it came into existence. However, insofar as it is born with sin, it belongs to the seed that was cursed after the disobedience of Adam.[12] Nonetheless, the corruption of nature caused by Adam's disobedience can be turned into good account by the riches of God's mercy.[13]

Now, arises the question of the moral status of infants in whom human will does not yet exist; it has only nature. That which brings the infants to the subjection of the devil is original sin. In Augustine's words:

> ...corruption is subjected to corruption, nature to nature, because the two are even in the devil; so whenever those who are beloved and elect are "delivered from the power of darkness" (Col.1:13) to which they are justly opposed, it is clear enough how great a gift is bestowed on the justified and good by the good God, who brings good even out of evil.[14]

Except for the sin of Adam, evil would not exist in infants. The corruption that has been accrued to the nature of infants can be subjected to the work of God. According to Augustine's explanation, the reason for the devil's dominion over nature is not because it is human nature, but it is sinful. Children are born in a sinful state because that state was transmitted to them by the first man, Adam. In other words, human nature is a creation of God, and as such, it is good, but it is the devil who corrupts it on account of original sin.[15]

In *City of God*, Augustine points out that God made the human person upright and consequently with a good will.[16] However, the first evil will, which preceded all human evil acts, was rather a kind of falling away from the work of God to its own works. If the human will had remained steadfast in the love of God, that higher and changeless good, it would not have turned away to find satisfaction in itself. The origin of evil will is pride, which is nothing but an undue exaltation of the soul.[17] Evil cannot

---

[11] Mt. 5:45
[12] *De Nuptiis*, Bk. I, 32.
[13] Rom. 9:33.
[14] *De Nuptiis*, Bk. I, Ch. 49.
[15] Ibid., Ch. 11.
[16] Ibid., Bk. XIV, 11.
[17] Ibid., 13.

exist without good because the nature in which evil exists, insofar as it is nature, is good.[18] The evil is removed, not by removing any nature or part of it but by "healing and correcting" that which had been vitiated and depraved.[19] This healing can be achieved only by God, who at first was able to give us this nature.

This explanation points us to the cause of evil in human nature. What we see here is a distinction between the work of God and the work of the devil. This distinction is useful in answering the Pelagian charges that "it is impossible for evil fruits to spring from so many good things, such as the bodies, sexes, and their unions...."[20] Augustine says that the body was created "honorably and well-pleasing," but the disobedience of the bodily members is due to the lust of the flesh, which is not from God. Human nature, whether born of wedlock or of adultery, is still the good creative work of God. One who denies the goodness of human nature denies the goodness of God. In Augustine's thought, there is a `making and remaking' of the nature which can be better understood in light of a `creation-fall- redemption' category. Accordingly, human nature that has become corrupt through original sin can be remade through the grace of Christ.

Throughout his writings, Augustine stresses the consequences of original sin for the descendants of Adam. He rightly argues, as scripture does, that it is through the offence of one man that death was introduced into the human race. On account of sin, the devil's work has penetrated the work of God. Original sin was the consequence of Adam's depraved will. When everything else is radically affected by the evil of original sin, God alone has the unchangeable, supreme goodness. He made all things good even before any evil came into existence.[21] The subject of original sin and its consequences for human race is treated with great attention in Augustine's discussion on the good of marriage and the evil of concupiscence.

The Good of Marriage and the Evil of Concupiscence

The good of marriage and the evil of concupiscence in human nature are clearly distinguished in Augustine's thought. The lust of the flesh, which he terms "the law in our members which wars against the law of our

---

[18] Ibid.
[19] Ibid.
[20] Ibid., Bk. I, 16.
[21] Ibid., 47.

mind,"[22] is not a fault of marriage. The goodness of marriage, as an honorable institution from God, is repeatedly affirmed by Augustine. Marital cohabitation or the bodily union of the spouses cannot be censured because of shameful lust associated with marriage. Contrasted are the good of the laudable union of the sexes and the evil of shameful lust.[23] In Augustine's thought, conjugal cohabitation has a shame-causing lust, but as long as this conjugal relationship is lawful, it finds a positive use in marriage. However, in an unlawful relationship, it has an evil use.

In other words, "the good of marriage is no more impeachable, because of original sin which is derived therefrom, than the evil of adultery and fornication can be excused, because of the natural good which is born of them...."[24] Therefore, one should neither excuse fornication on account of the good of the human nature produced from it nor censure marriage by reason of the evil of lust associated with the bodily union.

Offspring, Fidelity, and Marriage Bond

One can observe in Augustine's writings a well-developed theology of marriage, in which he consistently affirms the goodness of marriage, for which he identifies at least three good aspects that can be explained in the following way. The chief good of marriage is the procreation of children, and husband and wife become partners in a conjugal relationship. What is desired in a Christian marriage is the procreation of children, and not the gratification of lust. The role of faith in accomplishing this objective is significant because Augustine attaches much importance to the *motif* of salvation, in which faith is an inevitable element.

The purpose of procreation has an extended meaning in the context of marriage, namely, children are to be generated for the ultimate purpose of regenerating them in the grace of Christ.[25] What are born in original sin as "children of the world" are to be born again to become the "children of God." They are to be generated so as to be transferred from being "members of the first man" to being "members of Christ." Whenever the desire for the regeneration of children is ignored, there is no true chastity.

The notion of chastity is undergirded by faith in God and a hope for the conversion of children.[26] Chastity is a virtue, and every virtue has its

---

[22] Rom. 7:23
[23] *De Nuptiis*, Bk. I, 36.
[24] Ibid.
[25] Ibid., Bk. I, 5 (IV).
[26] Ibid., 4, 5.

seat in the soul and is expressed by the body. Therefore, the body cannot be said to be chaste when the soul is committing fornication. True faith in God is the foundation of true chastity, and for this reason, there is "no true chastity, conjugal, or vidual, or virginal except that which it devotes itself to faith."[27] In the words of St. Paul, "Whatsoever is not of faith is sin"[28] and "Without faith it is impossible to please God."[29]

The chastity of the unbeliever raises a problem. The role of faith in chastity is an essential element in Augustine's thought. Therefore, he rules out the possibility of genuine chastity in unbelievers. To state this position more positively in Augustinian terms, "only a believer can be a truly chaste person."[30] Those unbelievers who are dealing in matters of conjugal chastity are devoid of faith. Their motive is to either please others or to avoid troubles. In such cases, sins are not really restrained, but "some sins are overpowered by other sins."[31] Therefore, no one is really chaste except in the context of faith and devotion to the true God.

In considering further the Augustinian distinction, one may say that whereas procreation is good, concupiscence is evil. Shame is associated with sexual union, which is evil in nature, but the good of marriage cannot be affected by this evil. It is like the attainment of some good object by a lame person. This attainment is not evil because of the lameness, and the lameness is not good because of the goodness of the attainment. Similarly, the goodness of marriage ought not to be condemned because of concupiscence, and the evil of concupiscence should not be praised because of the good of marriage. Conjugal cohabitation is not evil where there is sanctity and honor[32] in the marriage relationship and where there is a genuine desire on the part of the parents for the salvation of the children. He who holds to the salvation *motif* cannot be said to possess his vessel in the "disease of desire," but in sanctification and honor.[33] The governing intent of marriage is to please God.[34]

The remaining good aspects of marriage are conjugal fidelity (*fides*) and the bond of marriage (*sacramentum*). Augustine sees the marriage of

---

[27] Ibid.
[28] Rom. 14:23
[29] Heb. 11:16
[30] *De Nuptiis*, Ch. 4.
[31] Ibid.
[32] I Thess. 4:3-5
[33] Augustine views concupiscence as a disease. See *De Nuptiis*, Bk. I.9.
[34] Heb. 11:4-6

Joseph and Mary as the perfect example of the presence of all of these blessings. In this marriage, there was no carnal lust, but there was conjugal fidelity because of which they were called the parents of Christ.[35] There was fidelity because there was no adultery. Because there was the bond of marriage, there was no divorce. In this unique relationship, there was neither concupiscence nor nuptial cohabitation. He who was to be born without sin should not be made in sinful flesh, but in the likeness of sinful flesh.[36] What Augustine says is that Christ could not possibly have been made in sinful flesh itself without the evil of concupiscence. He who is born of sexual union is born of sinful flesh, and that alone which was not born of sexual intercourse was not sinful flesh.[37]

Conjugal sexual union in the context of procreation is not sin. In Augustine's view, the good-will of the mind, namely, generating children for regeneration should lead the ensuing bodily pleasures, and not vice versa. In this situation, concupiscence, which he terms the "blow of the sin," is brought back to the use of procreation. He points out that

> this blow has a certain prurient activity which plays the king in the foul indulgences of adultery, and fornication, and lasciviousness and uncleanness; Whilst in the indispensable duties of the marriage state, it exhibits the docility of the slave.[38]

He makes the distinction very clear by adding that in the one case, it is "condemned as the shameful effrontery of so violent a master," and in the other, it receives "modest praise as the honest service of so submissive an attendant".[39] Concupiscence is not in itself the good of the marriage institution; it is evil. It is obscenity in sinful men, and a necessity in procreant parents. Concupiscence is the accident of original sin. Augustine points out those bodily organs, as created by God for the purpose of procreation, were not a cause of shame before the first sin of Adam. The good creation of God is to be distinguished from the evil of original sin. Sin did not originate from the goodness of marriage.[40]

According to Augustine, sexual union of married couples should be legitimized by the desire for the propagation of children. In other words, sexual union apart from this chief purpose of marriage cannot be

---

[35] Lk. 2:41
[36] Rom. 8:3
[37] *De Nuptiis*, Bk. I, 13.
[38] Ibid.
[39] Ibid.
[40] Ibid., 19, 23.

justified.⁴¹ The procreation of children against the will and desire of couples is a "criminal conduct" under the disguise of marriage. Here, Augustine attacks the idea of contraception, which for him is lustful cruelty. He says:

> Sometimes, indeed, this lustful cruelty, or, if you please, cruel lust, resorts to such extravagant methods as to use poisonous drugs to secure barrenness; or else, if unsuccessful in this, to destroy the conceived seed by some means previous to birth, preferring that its offspring should rather perish than receive vitality; or if it was advancing to life within the womb, should be slain before it was born.⁴²

According to Augustine, if both parties alike are so flagitious, they are not truly husband and wife. But if the two are not alike in such sin, the woman is the husband's harlot or the man the wife's adulterer.⁴³

Human Nature and Marriage in Relation to Original Sin

The doctrine of original sin has a dominant place in Augustine's thinking. The subjects of human nature, marriage, and concupiscence cannot be discussed without this doctrine.⁴⁴ The doctrines of original sin and grace can be called two pillars of his theological system. However, as Paul Rigby points out, the former is not derived from the latter; rather, the two doctrines are the face and counter-face of the same truth drawn from the same experience.⁴⁵

In his treatises on marriage and concupiscence, Augustine charges the Pelagians with trying to get rid of original sin by their praise of God's works. They maintain that marriage, which is good, is not the cause of evil, and as a result, no one could be born from it in a sinful state and

---

[41] Ibid., 17.
[42] Ibid., 17 (XV).
[43] Ibid.
[44] Although the pre-Augustinian church fathers understood the notion of original sin, it was St. Augustine who first formulated and developed the doctrine more fully. As in his other writings, the doctrine here expresses a fundamental dimension of human condition, and as such it serves as a foundational element in his theological anthropology.
[45] Paul Rigby, *Original Sin in Augustine's Confessions* (Ottawa: University of Ottawa Press, 1987), 7.

having need of a Savior.[46] Augustine says that sin, which is derived to children from marriage, does not belong to marriage but to the evil that accrues to the human agents, from whose union marriage comes into being. However, he has no problem with the Pelagians' praise of human nature, human seed, marriage and sexual union, and offspring. The body and all the natural endowments that are implanted in the soul, even in sinful individuals, are still God's gift. In making the distinction between good and evil, he shows that "the evil of shameful lust can exist without marriage and marriage might have been without it."[47] Marriage cannot exist without concupiscence, although concupiscence may exist without marriage.[48] Therefore, the evil in question does not accrue to marriage from its own God-given institution, but from the first transgression of Adam.

In response to the writings of Julian, Augustine asserts that the doctrine of original sin and the corruption of the human nature are due to sin. In the first place, Julian argues that cohabitation rightly used is good, and what is born from it is good. He states that children born in wedlock are by nature good, because the apostle shows the "use of the woman to be both natural, and in its way, laudable."[49] However, the excess of concupiscence is punishable.

Julian draws the conclusion that marriage is good, and the children born of it, being God's good work, are good and cannot be evil.[50] Because marriage is good, original sin cannot come through marriage. He contends that a good tree cannot produce evil fruit. According to Julian:

> Certainly if evil is contracted from marriage, it may be blamed, nay, cannot be excused; and you [Augustine] place under the devil's power its work and fruit, because everything which is the cause of evil is itself without good.[51]

In the second place, Julian argues that if sin comes by birth, all married people deserve condemnation. Because man is made by God, and the

---

[46] *De Nuptiis*, Bk. II, 42.
[47] Ibid., Bk. I, 42.
[48] The lust of the flesh can exist outside the marriage state as it may cause adultery and chambering.
[49] *De Nuptiis*, Bk. II, 34 (XIX).
[50] Ibid.
[51] Quoted by Augustine, *De Nuptiis*, Bk II, 41 (XXVI).

husband and wife are innocent, it is impossible for original sin to be derived from them.[52]

Augustine argues that either in wedlock or in fornication, what is born is born in sin.[53] An infant of either parentage may be delivered by the grace of Christ. Julian's use of the Gospel simile of the good tree (Mt. 7:18), as Augustine says, is a misinterpretation:

> Wherefore, if a human being is said to be the fruit of marriage, in the sense of a good fruit of a good tree, then undoubtedly a human being could never have been born in fornication. Therefore, his simile avails him nothing in elucidating the question, because marriage is not the cause of the sin which is transmitted in the natural birth, and atoned for in the new birth; but the voluntary transgression of the first man is the cause of original sin.[54]

The Pelagian interpretation of the doctrine of original sin is markedly different from that of Augustine. Pelagius teaches that the descendants of Adam sinned by imitating Adam and that sin did not enter into the world by one man's sin, whereas Augustine proposes that original sin passed upon all by generation.[55] Pelagius says that "by the example of Adam's disobedience many sinned", and that " as long as they sin the way (Adam sinned), they die the way (he died).[56] He denies the imputation of Adam's guilt to his descendants. Augustine shows that Adam stood at a two-fold relationship, toward God and toward his descendants, and that the guilt of his sin, as the federal head of the human race, was imputed to all descendants. To look at this in terms of the covenantal relationship, God had made a covenant[57] with Adam, not only for himself, but also for his posterity. Therefore, every member of the human race, descending from him by ordinary generation, sinned in him and fell with him, in his first

---

[52] Ibid., 44 (XXVII).

[53] *De Nuptiis*, Bk. I, 39. Because God is the author of human nature, an infant born in either state is in some respect good. However, he derives some evil by reason of original sin.

[54] *De Nuptiis*, Bk. II, 43.

[55] Ibid., 45.

[56] T. S. de Bruyn, *Pelagius's Commentary on St. Paul's Epistle to the Romans: A Translation With Introduction and Notes* (Doctoral diss., Toronto, 1987), 125.

[57] "The uncircumcised man-child, whose flesh of his foreskin is not circumcised on the eighth day, his soul shall be cut off from his people; because he hath broken my covenant" (Gen.17:14). See *De Nuptiis*, Bk. II, 24 (XI).

transgression. This action resulted in the breaking of the divine covenant. What covenant could an eight-day-old infant have broken, except it is the covenant that Adam had broken? Therefore, circumcision was instituted as a sign of the righteousness of faith, as well as an act to cleanse infants of original sin, just as baptism was instituted for the renewal of the person.

Although the Pelagian view of sin, its conception, and particulars is different from the Augustinian view, it has one point of similarity, namely, that Pelagius also considers sin in relation to the law of God and regards it as a transgression of the law.[58] Augustine stresses the fact that because of original sin every individual is born in sin and, therefore, is in the devil's power, unless he or she is regenerated in Christ.[59]

Augustine sees original sin as integral and radical as it penetrates and embraces every reality. It is the "great sin of Adam" whereby the devil inflicted a great wound to a "vastly wider and deeper extent than are the sins which are known amongst men."[60] The sin of Adam has a deteriorating effect on human nature, and this sin not only makes one a sinner but also makes one generate children who are sinners. Here also, his distinction between the good of human nature and its corruption due to the fall of Adam becomes well defined. The corruption that has accrued to human nature is something like a weakness or ailing of the body that keeps reproducing in the human descendants. Consequently, what believing parents transmit to their carnal offspring is the condition of their own carnal births, not that of their spiritual new birth.[61]

The cause of original sin in infants may be traced back to the evil willfully committed by Adam, and sin was derived from a nature thus corrupted. Since all have sinned in Adam, all have died in him. The origin and rise of sin in the human race can be attributed to nothing other than the sin and fall of the first man. The Pelagians argue that Adam was the first to sin, but anyone who wished afterwards to commit sin found an example in him for sinning. This means sin did not *pass* from Adam to all human beings by birth but by the *imitation* of this one sin.[62] Augustine

---

[58] Louis Berkhof, *Systematic Theology* (Grand Rapids: Eerdmans Publishing Co., 1949), 233.
[59] *De Nuptiis*, Bk. II, 25.
[60] Ibid., 57 (XXXIV).
[61] Ibid., 37.
[62] Ibid., 45.

rejects this view in his argument that original sin is passed upon the entire human race by natural generation.[63]

The doctrine of original sin is a scriptural truth that St. Augustine so ably expounds. Expounding on the Epistle of Paul to the Romans, he shows that in Adam all sinned, and many are dead, because of the offence of the first man.[64]

A major consequence of the sin of Adam is the introduction of death into the world. Death reigned in the likeness of transgression. Even those who did not sin still died "because of their origin in the mortality of Adam."[65] In the context of the reign of death, the grace of Christ comes to aid us in two ways. *First*, although death reigns for the time being, grace abounds much more so that it grants eternal life. *Second*, in Adam, one sin was condemned, but by the grace of the Lord many sins were forgiven.[66] The free gift delivers us not only from original sin but also from our actual sins committed by the motion of our own wills.[67] Here, a further distinction has been made between original sin and actual sin.

Augustine contrasts the work of Adam with the work of Christ. One brought condemnation and placed humanity under the power of the devil; the other brought justification and eternal life. The person born of whatever parentage is sinful because of Adam, but he or she is capable of redemption because of Christ.

On account of original sin and the corruption of human nature, `children of wrath' are born even in holy matrimony. Even in lawful and just marriages, children of wrath, and not children of God, are born. What is born of the lust of the flesh is born of the world, and they are born of God only when they are born again of water and of the Spirit.[68] This is an example of salvation *motif* that is found often in the works of Augustine. The guilt of concupiscence is remitted by regeneration alone, even as natural generation contracts it.[69] Of the necessity of regeneration, he has this to say:

---

[63] Ibid.
[64] Rom. 5.
[65] *Augustine on Romans: Propositions from the Epistle to the Romans*, text and trans. by Paula Fredriksen Landes (California: Scholars Press, 1982), 9.
[66] *De Nuptiis*, Bk. II, 11.
[67] Ibid., 46.
[68] Jn. 3:5
[69] *De Nuptiis*, Bk. I, 21. Because of the *motif* of salvation that stems from the fundamental understanding of creation-fall-regeneration, some writers interpret Augustine as the `theologian of cultural transformation'. Accordingly, Christ is the transformer of culture in the sense that He redirects, reinvigorates, and

> What, then, is generated must be regenerated, in order that likewise since it cannot be otherwise, what has been contracted may be remitted. It is, no doubt, very wonderful that what has been remitted in the parent should still be contracted in the offspring; but nevertheless such is the case....It is a wonderful thing, then, how those who have been delivered by grace from the bondage of sin, should still beget those who are tied and bound by the self-same chain, and who require the same process of loosening?[70]

For Augustine, this situation is like the embryo of the wild olive latently existing in the true olive. In the same manner, what is produced either by a righteous parent or a sinner is a sinner, notwithstanding the great differences that exist between the righteous and the sinner. The infant is born a sinner not as yet in act, but in guilt. He is human from the Creator, but he is a captive of the destroyer, and, therefore, he needs a redeemer. The state of captivity into which infants are born to parents who themselves have been delivered from it is a proof of original sin.

Role of Concupiscence in Sin

Sin is the origin of all shameful concupiscence, and it is sin that caused the first parents to be ashamed of their nakedness, and this shame never existed before the first sin of Adam.[71] Augustine's discussion of this topic is concerned more about the shameful motion of the organs of generation than about the motion of bodies as such. Concupiscence need not have been necessary for the act of procreation. The concerned organs of generation could have obeyed the human will just as a foot, arm, finger, or any other part of the body that accomplishes a task by the direction of the will without the lascivious heat or the ardor of lust.[72]

---

regenerates that life of the human person expressed in all human works, which in present actuality is the perverted and corrupted exercise of a fundamentally good nature. For example, see Richard H. Niebuhr, *Christ and Culture* (New York: Harper & Brothers, 1951), 208, 209.

[70] Ibid.

[71] Ibid., 26.

[72] Ibid., Bk. II, 53. In *Against Julian*, he says that the "unseemly movement...would not have existed in marriage if men had not sinned," which seems to be saying that there would have been lustless, soft erections in Paradise, generated at will and capable of intercourse without destroying the woman's virginity. See Joyce E. Salisbury, *Church Fathers, Independent Virgins* (London and New York: Verso,

This shameful concupiscence is not itself sin in the marriage relationship of the regenerate parents, provided they do not "consent to illicit works" and "do not apply their members by the presiding minds to perpetrate such deeds."[73] Nonetheless, this shameful concupiscence is evil because of how it arose from sin, but this sin is venial in the regenerate parents who make a right use of this evil for the good of marriage.

Augustine does not identify original sin with concupiscence. For him, concupiscence is only one of the effects of the fall of the first parents, although it is quite intimately connected with original sin. In no case does concupiscence happen to the human nature except from sin.[74] Now from this concupiscence, whatever is born by natural birth is bound by original sin, unless it is born again in Christ, who was born without concupiscence. Augustine explains in the following way the sense by which concupiscence is called sin:

> Inasmuch, however, as by a certain manner of speech it is called sin, since it arose from sin, and, when it has the upper hand, produces sin, the guilt of it prevails in the natural man; but this guilt, by Christ's grace through the remission of all sins, is not suffered to prevail in the regenerate man, if he does not yield obedience to it whenever it urges him to the commission of evil.
>
> As arising from sin, it is, I say, called sin, although in the regenerate it is not actually sin; and it has this designation applied to it, just as speech with the tongue produces is itself called "*tongue;*" and just as the word "*hand*" is used in the sense of writing, which the hand produces. In the same way concupiscence is called sin, as producing sin when it conquers the will: so to cold and frost the epithet "*sluggish*" is given; not as arising from, but as productive of, sluggishness, benumbing us, in fact.[75]

For Augustine, concupiscence is original sin in the same way that ignorance or even death is, that is in virtue of that metonymy that identifies effects with their causes.[76] Concupiscence has an inclination to sin, and, thus, it manifests the characteristic of moral imperfection, which is a reason for calling it sin.

1991), 45.
[73] Ibid., Bk. I, 25.
[74] Ibid., Bk. II, 27.
[75] Ibid., Bk. I, 25.
[76] See also Portalie, *op. cit.*, 208.

Two points that Augustine makes about concupiscence should be noted here. *First*, concupiscence remains in its entirety after baptism,[77] and, *second*, original sin is destroyed. This raises a question: If original sin is identified with concupiscence, how can original sin be destroyed and obliterated while concupiscence remains? The answer is that it is forgiven so as to be no longer a sin. It is no longer imputed.[78] The guilt of concupiscence is taken away, but it still remains "until our entire infirmity is healed by the advancing renewal of our inner man, day by day, when at last our outward man shall be clothed with incorruption."[79] After baptism, concupiscence remains as nothing more than a certain affection of an evil quality, such as languor after recovery from disease. As Eugene Portalie observes, if the nonimputation of concupiscence totally destroys the entire sin, then, since concupiscence remains, the only explanation must be that sin is not constituted by concupiscence but by the moral imputation of concupiscence.[80]

In the treatment of concupiscence, Augustine distinguishes between the physical reality of concupiscence, namely, its inclination towards evil, and the guilt of concupiscence, namely, its moral imputability. This moral imputability of concupiscence is that share of responsibility morally imputed to each child of Adam, rendering a person responsible for the presence of this evil within him or her. Thus, each individual becomes the author of this concupiscence because of his or her moral participation in the sin of Adam. Portalie expresses this very well:

> As long as this moral union of our responsibility is joined to that of Adam, God will see in us, with a legitimate displeasure and hostility, this rebellion of the senses. (The same must be said of ignorance and death.) This moral voluntareity, this culpability, is by itself precisely and formally the whole essence of original sin; concupiscence, ignorance, and so forth are properly its effects. Thus, when God in baptism pardons this moral voluntareity which makes us responsible for the sin of Adam, original sin is totally forgiven. Concupiscence, however, remains, but no longer implies guilt in us since the sin has been forgiven: "It is...forgiven so...as to be no longer a sin."[81]

---

[77] *De Nuptiis*, Bk. I, 28. Carnal concupiscence is remitted in baptism, not so that it is put out of existence, but so that it is not to be imputed for sin.
[78] Portalie, 209; *De Nuptiis*, Bk. I, 28.
[79] *De Nuptiis*, Bk. I, 28.
[80] Portalie, 209.
[81] Portalie, 210; *De Nuptiis*, Bk. I, 32, 54.

Concluding Critical Comments

St. Augustine's theology of marriage and sexuality has had a profound influence on the Church's attitude towards human sexuality. For some, his teaching is affirming of their view of human nature, marriage, and procreation, which are consistent with the teaching of the scriptures. For others, it is highly controversial in matters of homosexuality and contraception. This perspective is especially so nowadays, when the issues relating to the ordination of practicing homosexual persons to the priesthood have caused division in the contemporary Church. Augustine views homosexuality as an offence against God and nature. This is what we read in his *Confessions*:

> Crimes therefore which are offences against nature, are everywhere and always abominable and punishable. Such were those of the people of Sodom. If all nations were to do the like, they would stand guilty in the same degree before the same law, because it did not so make men that they should treat one another thus.[82]

Accordingly, acts that are contrary to nature are to be detested and punished everywhere. They are contrary to the divine purpose of sexuality, which is procreation.[83] This position faces serious criticisms from the proponents of same-sex union within the Christian church. For example, John McNeill, in his work[84] that has been described as a "vintage work in the evolving history of the relationship between gay people and institutional Christianity," stresses the positive character of homosexuality. According to him, "[h]omosexual love, although incapable of procreation, is certainly not doomed to fruitlessness."[85]

---

[82] *The Confessions of Saint Augustine*, trans. C. Bigg (London: Methuen & Co., 1898), 101-102.

[83] Scholastic thought was also largely influenced by the early church fathers, especially Saint Augustine. St. Thomas, for example, in his list of four *pecca contra naturam* (*Summa Theologica* II-II, Q. cliii, 3; Q. cliii; and Q. cliv. I), includes homosexual genital contact. Such "unnatural vices" or "sins against nature" are results of excessive lust that goes beyond the "order and mode of reason." These vices are particularly sinful because they occur in situations in which the created purpose of sexuality, procreation, cannot take place.

[84] John McNeill, *The Church and the Homosexual*, 3rd ed. (Boston: Beacon Press, 1988), 149.

[85] Ibid., 108.

Accordingly, the end of human sexuality is not the generation of children and their regeneration, but "mutual love" and "fulfillment" between the homosexual partners. Such homosexual love, he argues, has the character of a liberation to a truly spiritual fertility that otherwise would have been impossible.[86] Such voices are becoming increasingly louder in contemporary society, creating divisions within the mainline Christian churches. In the thought of St. Augustine, same-sex union is not liberative but enslaving.

There are also other theologians, who describe homosexuality as a malady. Karl Barth is an example:

> This is the physical, psychological and social sickness, the phenomenon of perversion, decadence and decay, which can emerge when man refuses to admit the validity of the divine command....But the decisive word of Christian ethics must consist in a warning against entering upon the whole way of life which can only end in the tragedy of concrete homosexuality.[87]

Augustine's understanding of conjugal cohabitation leads us to ask whether human sexuality can be separated from the objective of procreation. Can sexual union, quite apart from this task of matrimony, be considered legitimate? What about heterosexual couples who cannot have children? What is the role of sexual union in such cases?

Both the Roman Catholic and Anglican traditions basically agree on the `conceptional' and `relational' motives of coition.[88] Whereas the former is intended for procreation of children, the latter has the purpose of establishing the "one flesh" union about which the Bible teaches. These two aspects are not to be separated so that the one would exclude the other entirely and permanently. Can sexual union in lawfully married couples be understood as promoting the relational aspect we have just noted? Can sexual union be considered as a means of bringing with it its own joy, in the love of two human beings for one another?[89]

---

[86] Ibid.
[87] Karl Barth, *Church Dogmatics* III. 4 (Edinburgh: T & T Clark, 1961), 166.
[88] The Catholic position is stated in Michael J. Buckley, *Morality and the Homosexual* (Westminster: The Newman Press, 1959), 134. The Anglican position is related in D. S. Bailey, "Homosexuality and Christian Morals," *They Stand Apart*, J. Tudor Rees and Harvey V. Usill, eds (London: William Heinemann Lt., 1955), 49.
[89] Dietrich Bonhoeffer, *Ethics*, Eberhard Bethge, ed., trans. by Neville Horton Smith (New York: The Macmillan Co., 1965), 49. Bonhoeffer maintains that the

Whereas Augustine makes assertions on the usefulness of sexuality to meet the "natural needs" of the human persons, he does not emphasize the sociological or anthropological dimension of sexual relationship in the treatises. This, however, does not mean that he totally disregards these dimensions in his writings. In fact, he sees in the `man-woman' relationship what he calls the "first natural bond of human society."[90] What also needs to be stressed is the sociological dimension that sees marriage as a sexual fellowship. Sexuality is another dimension of human personality that is an expression of relationship to the other person. As Peter Brown explains, Augustine's view of marriage deliberately looks past the physicality of marital intercourse. Sexual desire still disquieted him, and it is seen as a "disruptive force" in humankind's present state.[91] Therefore, he never articulates the possibility that sexual pleasure might, in itself, enrich the relation between husband and wife.[92]

Marriage, according to Genesis 2:18 and Ephesians 5:21-33, has a mutual completing and perfecting of the partners through their union, which finds its strongest expression in sexual relationship. Although sexuality is directly biological, it is indirectly related to sociological, economic, and physical factors. Also as Johannes Gründel points out, sex and eros are not merely individual and personal; they are, as well, both public and intimate in character.[93] Therefore, in any society, sexuality is subject to social norms. If the social aspect of sexuality is not taken seriously, sexual behavior is directed to the partner in a merely functional way, that is, for the purpose of conception or for the satisfaction of desire. Either one amounts to a perverting of sexual powers, as their full meaning cannot be realized in a fleeting encounter.[94]

Finally, Augustine explicitly condemns all methods of contraception in *De Nuptiis et Concupiscence,* and what emerges from his discussion of these topics is relevant to the life of the Church.[95] The topic of

---

life of "the body assumes its full significance only with the fulfillment of its inherent claim to joy."

[90] *De Bono Conjugali,* I.

[91] Peter Brown, *The Body and Society: Men, Women and Sexual Renunciation in Early Christianity* (New York: Columbia University Press), 402.

[92] Ibid.

[93] Johannes Gründel, "Sexual Morality," *Encyclopedia of Theology,* Karl Rahner, ed (New York: Crossroad, 1975), 1575.

[94] Ibid., 1574.

[95] *De Nuptiis.,* Bk. I, 17.

contraception is not only a theological issue but also a political one. Augustine calls contraception a "criminal conduct" which runs against the true standard of holy matrimony.

The Christian Church has a moral task to provide sexual education to its members. Human sexuality, as a divine gift, affects the expressed behavior as well as mental acts of every human being; in fact, it provides identity and structure to the individual from the very beginning of existence. Sexuality as God's gift is fully acceptable to God. The Church must teach once again that sexual differences between man and woman are an intrinsic part of human constitution and that they cannot be viewed in isolation from what God has intended from the beginning, or abstracted from the totality of human personality. This truth is found at the core of divine revelation, and, therefore, serves as a foundational element in the Church's task of sexual education. Many of the contemporary debates and discussions do not give credence to God's revelation, and as such, they are antithetical to God's revealed will.

The contemporary Church is encountering, on the one hand, an ever-increasing tide of "pro-choice" activities, which support contraception and abortion, and, on the other, a shortage of resources arising out of overpopulation, especially in the developing countries. It also faces many secular forces that seek to destroy the very foundation of the institution of marriage. In this predicament, the Christian church has much to learn from the frame of reference offered in the theology of St. Augustine.

BIBLIOGRAPHY

Augustine, Saint. *Confessions*, trans. Vernon J. Bourke, New York: Fathers of the Church, Inc., 1953.

-----*On Marriage and Concupiscence*, Books I & II, ed. Philip Schaff, *Nicene and Post-Nicene Fathers of the Christian Church*, vol. 5, Grand Rapids: Wm. B. Eerdmans, 1956.

-----*On the Good of Marriage*, trans. C. L. Cornish, ed. Philip Schaff, Buffalo

-----*The City of God*, Book XIV, *Augustine's Works*, Vol. 2, ed. Marcus Dods, Edinburgh: T & T Clark, 1872.

-----*On the Grace of Christ and on Original Sin*, ed. Philip Schaff, *Nicene and Post-Nicene Fathers*, Grand Rapids: Eerdmans, 1956.

Bailey, D. S. "Homosexuality and Christian Morals," *They Stand Apart*, J. Tudor Rees and Harvey V. Usill, eds, London: William Heinemann Ltd., 1955.

Barth, Karl. *Church Dogmatics* III.4, Edinburgh: T & T Clark, 1961.

Bentivegna, J. "Julian of Eclanum," *New Catholic Encyclopedia*, Vol.8, William J. McDonald, ed., Washington, D.C.: The Catholic University of America, 1966.

Berkhof, Louis. *Systematic Theology*, Grand Rapids: Eerdmans Publishing Co., 1949.

Bonhoeffer, Dietrich. *Ethics*, Eberhard Bethge, ed, trans. Neville Horton Smith New York: The Macmillan Co., 1965.

Brown, Peter R. *Augustine of Hippo: A Biography*, London: Faber & Faber, 1967.

-----*The Body and Society: Men, Women, and Sexual Renunciation Early Christianity*, New York: Columbia University Press, 1988.

Buckley, Michael. *Morality and the Homosexual*, Westminster: The Newman Press, 1959.

Burns, Paul C. "Julian of Eclanum," *Encyclopedia of Early Christianity*, Everett Ferguson, ed, New York: Garland Publishing Co., 1990.

de Bruyn, T. S. *Pelagius's Commentary on Romans*, A Translation with Introduction and Notes, Doctoral Thesis, Toronto, 1987.

Landes, Paula. *Augustine on Romans: Propositions from the Epistle to the Romans*, text and translation, California: Scholars Press, 1982.

MacNeill, John. *The Church and the Homosexual*, 3rd ed., Boston: Beacon Press, 1988.

McWilliam, Joanne."Pelagian, Pelagianism," *Encyclopedia of Early Christianity*, Everett Ferguson, ed, New York: Garland Publishing Co., 1990.

Niebuhr, Richard H. *Christ and Culture*, New York: Harper & Brothers, 1951.

Portalie, Eugene. *A Guide to the Thought of Saint Augustine*, trans. Ralph J. Bastian, London: Burns & Oates, 1960.

Rahner, Karl. ed., *Encyclopedia of Christianity*, New York: Crossroad, 1975.

Rigby, Paul. *Original Sin in Augustine's Confessions*, Ottawa: University of Ottawa Press, 1987.

Salisbury, Joyce. E. *Church Fathers, Independent Virgins*, New York: Verso, 1991

Chapter Two

ROBERTO DE NOBILI

Christ and Culture in Theological Method

Roberto De Nobili (1577-1656) was a 17th-century Italian Jesuit missionary to India. Known for his remarkable intellectual ability and theological acumen, he was a missionary to the Brahmins of South India. Perhaps, no missionary before or after him has received in India such great admiration and acclaim for the contributions made to the areas of theology, inter-religious dialogue, linguistics, and human culture. Missiologists see him as the first Western missionary to understand Hinduism from its primary sources and interpret its doctrines with a remarkable degree of knowledge and lucidity. Those who would undertake to study De Nobili's life and work will find in it invaluable intellectual and cultural resources to inform their own cross-cultural communication of the Gospel in today's world.

The purpose of this study[1] is to learn from the life of De Nobili some cross-cultural and inter-religious lessons that are useful in our own missiological engagement of Hindu doctrines and worldview. His interpretation of Hindu belief system in the colonial cultural setting will be the central theme we will be examining here. The questions and issues that De Nobili faced in his context are still alive in today's theological circles, where the salvific nature of non-Christian religions and the uniqueness of the Christian revelation have been discussed and debated.

---

[1]Roberto De Nobili has written approximately fifty books in Indian languages, in addition to many letters and treatises in Portuguese, Italian, and Latin. Some works are not extant, and some not readily accessible to readers in the West. The works of scholars such as S. Rajamanickam, S. Arokiasamy, D.Yesudhas, and Vincent Cronin have been important sources for researchers, including the present writer, who has made frequent references to their works.

Christianity and the 17th Century Colonialism: A Contextual Overview

The relationship of Christianity to Western colonialism has been a much-debated topic in India for a long time. During the period from 1498 to 1947 (from Vasco Da Gama to India's independence), India was a favorite destination for European colonizers, for it was during this period that India came in contact with several Western nations, such as Portugal, France, Denmark, and Britain. The significance of this period for the future development of Christian missions in that country can never be overestimated. When De Nobili arrived in South India in 1606, the region from Goa to the Malabar Coast had a reasonably strong Jesuit missionary presence, but the progress of the mission had been slow. His arrival at the Madurai Mission began to energize the life of the Roman Catholic Church in Goa, giving it a new force for missionary work. From the time of Francis Xavier who worked there from 1534, Goa had been the center of colonial powers, with the church's authority extending to the Far East.

De Nobili worked in the Portuguese colonial context, and the characteristics of this era are worth mentioning. *First*, there was an inseparable link between Western Christianity and the Portuguese colonialism in Goa. The Portuguese control of Goa and Madurai, with its mission of converting the Hindus to Christianity, became an inter-religious problem. The Christianization of the newly 'discovered' lands in Asia was financed by the king. The Portuguese work was based on the Bulls of Calixtus III, Nicholas V, and Alexander VI. The kings of Portugal and Spain had the task of Christianizing the new territories allotted to them.[2]

Second, for the Portuguese, commercial gain from the region was as important as the task of converting the people. With this twin-purpose (humorously termed in India "pepper and souls") in mind, they made relentless efforts to obtain spices and tried to control the sea-born trade of India. Their ambition was to seize the trade from the Arabs and Italians and divert it to Lisbon.[3]

Third, most Christian missionary undertakings received strong support from the colonial rulers. This support was a result of a very close identification of Western imperialism with its Christian missions in India.

---

[2] For a detailed presentation of the colonial situation of this era, see K. M. Panikkar, *Asia and Western Dominance* (London: George Allen & Unwin, 1953), 280.
[3] Kenneth Scott Latourette, A *History of the Expansion of Christianity*, vol. 3 (New York and London: Harper & Brothers, 1939), 249.

As Latourette points out, the Portuguese power and greed either helped or embarrassed the Roman Catholic missions during this period by conquering locations for missionaries' works in Goa.[4] Consequently, Christianity's association with colonialism has been a controversial topic in India and other Asian countries,[5] which led some to describe Christian mission as the "hunting dog of western imperialism."[6]

Fourth, the Portuguese Viceroy's religious zeal had led to the destruction of many Hindu temples in 1540, and the wealth of these temples had been turned over to religious societies, like the Franciscans. Practices of this kind, according to Stephen Neill, were based on a medieval law that whenever a religious establishment could no longer meet its 'founding-purpose,' its possession could be reallocated for good purposes. In England, this law became handy to Henry VIII for the dissolution of monasteries.[7]

Finally, the cruelty inflicted on the colonized in the Portuguese conquest of Goa, Malacca, and Ormuz gave Christianity a bad name among the people. Many years after the conquest, a missionary named Nicolas Lancilotto, who wrote from Goa on December 5, 1550, had this to say:

> Whereas all those who came out here were soldiers, who went about conquering lands and enslaving people, these same soldiers began to baptize the said people whom they enslaved without any respect and reverence for the sacrament, and without any catechizing or indoctrination. And since the inhabitants of these countries are very miserable, poor and cowardly, some were baptized through fear, others through worldly gain, and others for filthy and disgusting reasons which need not mention.[8]

---

[4] Ibid.

[5] For example, this association is the "historic problem for Christianity in China today," according to Zhuo Xinping, deputy director of the Chinese Academy of Social Sciences. In his opinion, those who would like to examine religious freedom in China must first examine this enduring problem. See "China Blames Christians," *The Toronto Star*, Saturday 28, 1986, L 14.

[6] A. J. Temu, *British Protestant Missions* (London: Longman, 1972), 132. Also, for a discussion of the historical background of Christian missions and Colonialism, see Lal Dena, *Christian Missions and Colonialism: A Study of Missionary Movement in Northeast India With Particular Reference to Manipur and the Lushai Hills 1894-1947* (Shillong: Vendrame Institute, 1988), 1-30.

[7] Stephen Neill, *Colonialism and Christian Missions* (London: Lutterworth Press, 1966), 72.

[8] Ibid.

During this period, Hindus within the Portuguese territory were forced to accept Christianity, and, as Latourette again points out, in some instances, the hope of Portuguese protection encouraged the requests for baptism. [9] The interdependence of Christian missionary work and aggressive imperialism produced several political complications.[10] The cruelty inflicted on the people through the Portuguese conquest and the "cultural superiority which the missionaries perhaps unconsciously introduced in India are not easily forgotten."[11]

However, De Nobili refused to have any link between his work and colonial power, for the Christian church would have had little success if it had been kept to its European framework. His intellectual preparation at home provided him with invaluable tools for his mission among the Hindus.

De Nobili's Intellectual Preparation

De Nobili was born in 1577 in Rome to Pier Francesco and Clarice in a Roman noble family. The family descended from Emperor Otho III, the heritage of which would later help him claim the status of a *rajah sanyasi* among the Brahmins of South India. After the death of his father in 1593, he came under the guardianship of his cousin Cardinal Francesco Sforza. Upon completing studies at Roman College, he entered in 1596 the Jesuit novitiate in Naples, where he received education in theology and philosophy. He was ordained in 1600. The study of the patristic and scholastic works, as Gispert-Sauch notes, prepared him for the work in India.[12] Furthermore, in order to understand the missionary methods and practices used overseas, De Nobili would read letters that missionaries had sent to Europe. He also took time to familiarize himself with the work of Matteo Ricci. The intellectual preparation at home yielded knowledge and insights that would help his adaptation to the Hindu culture. It is said that De Nobili's approach to the Brahmins was more positive than that of his predecessor Francis Xavier.[13]

---

[9] Latourette, 249.
[10] K. M. Panikkar, *Asia and Western Dominance* (New York: The John Day Company/Collier Books, 1969), 297.
[11] Ibid.
[12] G. Gispert-Sauch, S.J. "Robert De Nobili and Hinduism," *God's Word Among Men: Papers in Honor of Fr. Joseph Putz, S.J.* (New Delhi: Vidyajyoti, 1973).
[13] Francis Xavier saw the Brahmins as the "most perverse people in the world, and of them was written the Psalmist's prayer: *De gente non sancta, ab homine*

De Nobili and the Indian Social Context

Language and Culture

Training in language and culture is essential to effective communication of the Gospel in any culture. Unlike his European contemporaries, De Nobili mastered several languages of India. His understanding of Sanskrit was profound. He wrote in each of these languages theological treatises that became significant resources for future missionaries. He was called the "father of Tamil prose," and his mastery of that language earned him the title *Tattuva Boddagar* (Teacher of philosophy). No missionary can engage the Brahmins without high proficiency in Sanskrit, the sacred language of the *Vedas*. The mastery of Sanskrit was the key to opening the complex religion and philosophy of the people. He was seen as an Oriental scholar, being the first European to study Sanskrit.[14] His work *Gnanopadesam* has the style of a *Summa Theologica,* which engages weighty theological concepts and themes. The theological discourses were loaded with vivid and lucid expressions of Tamil and Sanskrit and were replete with multi-layered clauses. This unusual linguistic mastery enabled him to articulate in these languages a fresh vision of the Christian faith that the Hindu Brahmins could understand.

The language barrier is the greatest cross-cultural challenge in the communication of the Gospel. The proclamation of the Christian message in another culture can be effective only when the message is translated into the language of the hearer. The language is a vehicle of religious and cultural presuppositions, which include the basic tenets of culture or subculture.[15] De Nobili's linguistic capability is an inspiring lesson for all missionaries to India. Many Western missionaries have arrived in India with little or no preparation in linguistics, philosophy, and religions of the country. For a long time, these missionaries have dismissed Indian religions and philosophies as the "devil's work." De Nobili bridged the

---

iniquo et doloso erue me. They do not know what it is to tell the truth but for ever plot how to lie subtly and deceive their poor ignorant followers.... Were it not for these Brahmins all the heathens would be converted." Quoted by Vincent Cronin, *A Pearl to India: The Life of Roberto De Nobili* (London: Rupert Hart-Davis, 1959), 84.

[14] For a detailed understanding of his literary and linguistic achievements, see S. Rajamanickam, *The First Oriental Scholar* (Tirunelveli: De Nobili Research Institute, 1972).

[15] Eugene Nida and William D. Reyburn, *Meaning Across Cultures* (Maryknoll: Orbis, 1981), 10.

gap between the European culture and the host culture by his knowledge of languages, which gave him considerable success in relating to the Hindus because he was able to view the Christian message through the Hindu eye, through its cultural presuppositions and belief systems.

The linguistic and cultural knowledge facilitated his easy entry into the complex Hindu world, its religious aspirations,[16] and the incessant search for *moksha*. He studied their religious practices of penance, ceremonies, and ablutions, aimed at achieving the bliss. Their quest for spirituality became his point of departure in initiating dialogues with the Brahmins. De Nobili considered such a religious quest to be extraordinary and exceptional. Moreover, he understood that the Brahmins were intelligent, and were committed to religious principles. He acquired detailed knowledge of the Brahmins through the study of the *Vedas* and the *Upanishads*,[17] which became important tools for his theological method known as "adaptation." In a 1609 letter to Fr. A. Laerzio, De Nobili commented on the knowledge of the Brahmins:

> We think that those men have no knowledge. I can assure you that they are far from [such a state]; just now I am reading one of their books which is a real philosophical treatise almost with the same terminology as those Istudied in Rome, although fundamentally their philosophy is very different from ours.[18]

An important note is that De Nobili did not reject the Hindu religion and philosophy as the 'work of the devil,' a mistake many Western missionaries have made over the years. Rather, he sought to understand and to interpret them from a Christian perspective. He began to use the terms *civilis cultus* and *mos politicus* to mean what is merely a positive human way of conceiving the socio-cultural realities that are acceptable and are to be kept as far as possible.[19] This distinction became useful in expressing the common concerns of Christianity and Hinduism.

---

[16] Reference has been made to the unceasing quest for the perfection of the human person. The doctrine of *Sadhana* is such an effort to achieve oneness with the Absolute. Cf., Troy Organ, *The Hindu Quest for the Perfection of Man* (Ohio: Ohio University Press, 1970), 59.
[17] The *Vedas* are the earliest and the most sacred texts in Hinduism and the *Upanishads* are philosophical writings, which constitute the earliest metaphysical inquiry into the nature and character of Brahman, atman, and the physical world.
[18] Quoted by Hambye, *op.cit.*, 327.
[19] *Apologia*, I, 63, 73.

What we can learn from his method is this: missionaries should study Hindu scriptures so that they can make an educated distinction between what is morally and socially good and what is superstitious and unintelligent. Cultural tools can be used in contextualizing Christian worship, and it is quite legitimate to identify and use the terms and ideas that are common to all religious people. A proper understanding of such similarities between the two can then be used in forming new rites, which eventually aid in the meaningful presentation of Christianity in the cultural context. To use the language of Bernard Lonergan,[20] it is wrong to view the alien culture as an enemy of the Gospel that must be eradicated before the planting of the church. When the church makes adaptations by grasping and mastering the languages and religions of the culture, that culture will offer essential frameworks for the natural development of the message.

The Interpretation of Caste System as a Social Reality

The caste system[21] practiced in India has been a vexing problem for Western missionaries and colonial rulers alike. This hierarchical system is based on certain religious beliefs with far-reaching social implications for the entire society, including the Church. Questions have been posed about what to do with a deep-rooted stratification of society, where people have been viewed in terms of their inherited and inalienable status. How will the Church address the polarity between the "pure" Brahmins and the "polluted" Untouchables? How does the Church bring them together once they are converted to Christianity? Do people see caste distinction as an "exclusion from" or a "belonging to"?

The caste system has been an integral part of Indian society, and De Nobili believed that the missionaries did not come to abolish it; rather, they should use it in a creative way. Therefore, he has this advice for his successors:

> In whichever country the priest enters, he should keep guards against even venial sins, and walk on the path of perfection. But in each country there are customs which are not sinful. The priest should consider these and find out which custom is

---

[20] Bernard Lonergan, *Method in Theology*, 361-363. Cf. J. M. Thomas, "The Notion of Communications in the Theological Method of Bernard Lonergan," *Mission Today: A Journal of Missiological and Ecumenical Research*, 5 (2003): 42-43.
[21] The caste system places Brahmins at the top and Sudras at the bottom and in between them are the Kshatriyas and the Vaishyas.

harmful to the spread of the Faith, and of course he should avoid it. However, if he finds it very advantageous to the spread of the Faith, it is wise and just to take it up.[22]

Thus, in order to win the Brahmins to Christianity, he had to become one himself, [23] calling himself a *rajah sanyasi*. This approach is fundamental to the understanding of his method of "adaptation." Accordingly, the preacher can make use of the social customs of the people whom he has come to evangelize, and thus make himself all things to all people.[24] Consequently, he interpreted the caste system as "civil grades" of the Indian social structure, even though at conversion, the new Christian had to renounce all these caste-related obligations such as the thread worn on the breast, the tuft of hair, the use of sandalwood paste on the forehead, and ceremonial baths, which were essential to the Brahmin priests.

For De Nobili, to evangelize India was to evangelize the Brahmins first, because they exercised the highest religious and social authority in the land. He understood that the "Brahmins alone in India represent the intelligentsia and the teaching profession," which is another reason he focused his attention on them.[25]

As a *rajah sanyasi*, De Nobili wore the five-stranded thread, instead of the three-stranded one that the Brahmin priests wore. Three golden strands represented the Trinity, and two white strands symbolized the Body and the Soul of Christ; from the thread was hung a crucifix, which stood for Redemption. He contextualized the Brahmin custom, because "no practice, or custom, or habit which in itself contains any sin, has ever been disapproved or condemned by the Church, even though it were current among the gentiles [sic] as well, to whom in fact it owed its origin."[26]

He honored the Hindu civil structure by acknowledging the caste distinction and also honored the dignity of each caste in light of his

---

[22] *Dushana Dhikkaram* (Refutation of blasphemies), 1641, 493.
[23] Christianity must not be preached as an exported commodity from Europe, as Karl Rahner puts it in another context. See Karl Rahner, "Towards a Fundamental Theological Understanding of Vatican II," *Theological Studies*, Vol. 40 (Washington, DC: Georgetown University, 1979), 716 -727.
[24] *Adaptation*, ed S. Rajamanickam, S.J., (Tirunelveli: De Nobili Research Institute, 1971), 11. The works of Rajamanickam and Arokiasamy have been acknowledged here as helpful sources in understanding De Nobili's cultural anthropology.
[25] *Indian Customs*, Ch. XI (Tirunelveli: De Nobili Research Institute, 1972), 149.
[26] *Adaptation*, 37.

Christian view. Furthermore, in order to accommodate Christian converts from all castes, a church building was designed and built such that all could sit under the same roof and receive the sacraments from the same priest while satisfying the caste law of sitting apart from each other, in different wings of the same building.[27] This unusual method has brought him much criticism from almost all theologians and social reformers who studied his work. The social compromise was aimed at overcoming the barriers in a caste-ridden society. Even today, neither the Indian church nor the government has been able to find a permanent solution to the problem of caste distinction.

It is the task of every missionary to understand the customs existing in any given society. Each society has its own social customs, which can be used creatively to communicate the Gospel. This means that the Gospel is not to be preached in the idioms of the missionary. As Lonergan points out, to use the resources of one's own culture in another culture is not to communicate with the other but to remain locked up in one's own.[28] This is an important cross-cultural lesson for all missionaries.

The presentation of the superiority of the Christian message does not lead to an immediate negation of Hinduism and its teachings. It is a complex and inclusive religion that pervades the entire socio-cultural life of India. Many early missionaries who failed to penetrate its outer cultural layer reported a version of this religion without its foundational teachings based on the Vedas.[29] The cultural imperialism of the missionaries that resulted from the political supremacy and economic prosperity of the West came to bear upon their missionary attitude.[30]

The early Catholic missions to India were seen as an extension of the Portuguese colonial enterprise. De Nobili broke all ties with the Portuguese in order to shake off the stigma of being called a *Paranghi*, a derogatory name given to the Portuguese and their converts. This step helped improve the credibility of the church in Goa. Lamin Sanneh is right when he says that De Nobili was aware of the mistake of associating Christianity with the colonial power, because "the inevitable decline of the Portuguese power in India would leave the church helplessly exposed."[31]

---

[27] Savarimuthu Rajamanickam, *The First Oriental Scholar* (Tirunelveli: De Nobili Research Institute, St. Xavier's College, 1972), 63.
[28] Lonergan, 300.
[29] Organ, 9.
[30] Ibid., 79.
[31] Lamin Sanneh, *Translating the Message: The Missionary Impact on Culture* (New

De Nobili was instrumental in the conversion of many Hindus to Christianity in Madurai. He also helped create a vocabulary of religion that was linguistically acceptable to people. He had much to say about the concepts of God found in Hinduism and the religion's salvific claims.

On God and Salvation

The Concept of God: A Christian Clarification

Fundamental to the work of Christian mission in a culture like India is a Christian theology that clearly explains the concept of God. Such a theology has to be Trinitarian in nature in order to provide a Christological framework that is different from all the competing truth claims.

De Nobili saw the need for clearing the linguistic ground for a correct theological identity of God that is consistent with Christian revelation. The existing systematic study of God in Hinduism, namely, *Adhyatmika Sastra*,[32] did not have the necessary clarity. According to him, the writers "turn the science of philosophy into a sort of mystery, particularly with a very disconcerting process of speaking," which consists of "words without any link among them."[33]

The Brahmins had different schools of theology, but the kinds of language used in describing the concepts of God were vague, so De Nobili adopted whatever language was in agreement with the Christian revelation.

The theology of the *Gnanis* among the Brahmins was related to the Vedanta.[34] Its notion of one God who can be known by the light of reason was appealing to De Nobili. Consequently, he rejected the possibility of multiple gods, the teaching about *maya*, and the principle of an identical soul existing in all beings.[35] The *Gnanis* rejected the view that sacrifices to gods will bring salvation of soul. In support of this view, De Nobili cites a

---

York: Maryknoll, 1989), 100.
[32] *Indian Customs*, S. Rajamanickam, ed (Palayamkottai: De Nobili Research Institute, 1972), 29.
[33] Ibid.
[34] Ibid, 29, 30. Each *Veda* consists of three parts, namely, the *Mantras* or hymns, the *Brahmanas* or explanations of hymns, and the *Upanishads*, which come at the end of the *Veda*. The teaching that is based on the Veda is called *Vedanta*.
[35] The principle of 'sameness' (same substance) exists in all beings. In God, it is *Paramatma* and in the Atman it is called *Jivatma*.

Vedic text: "Not from sacrifices nor from the happiness of children, nor from riches, nor from free distribution of wealth do men obtain beatitude."[36]

He understood some Hindu attributes of God as consistent with the Christian revelation, namely, the oneness of God, the eternal existence of God, the self-existence God, and God being the beginning and end himself. The *Taittirya Upanishad* says that God is infinite knowledge.[37] And again, "God is spiritual in form" (*akasa sariram Brahma*). Another testimony of the *Taittiriya Upanishad* is well received by De Nobili: "Thou, say I, art God and brightness itself, thee God I say to be true, thee I say to be truth" (I.1.1).[38] However, he knew that a correct understanding of the nature of God alone does not merit one salvation.

There also are Hindu ideas about God that he rejected. *First*, any notion of sinful conduct[39] in God, as is found in the *Puranas*, should have consequences for the practice of *dharma*. Such conducts attributed to God would be morally confusing to people. Thus, one would not have fear of sin or shame.[40] *Second*, the belief that there exists in God a principle called *maya*, from which God created all things, is contrary to the Christian view of God. God does not take forms of created things, as has been taught in Hinduism. If God did, it would remove the distinction between God and creation and would lead one to the worship of creation. This is a problem among Hindus that is revealed in misdirected worship. Respecting the creature is one thing, and worshipping God is another thing;[41] the confusion of the two results from ignorance about the true nature of God. Since God is good and cannot do evil, no wrongs can be attributed to God.[42] He rejected the veracity of most of the *Puranas*, which contradicted reason and ethics. He rightly argued that God cannot do what is contrary to his nature.

---

[36] *Indian Customs*, 38. Sanskrit: "*Na karmana na prajaya dhanena tyagenaikena amrtatvam anasuh*" (Yajur Veda, Taittiriya Aranyaka, 10.10 3 a).
[37] *Jnanam anantam Brahma*, or *infinita intellect*, S. Radhakrishnan, trans., 2.1.1, 541.
[38] *Indian Customs*, 34.
[39] Reference has been made to the *Puranic* beliefs about gods collaborating in a kind of magic to destroy one another, gods who want sacrifices on the basis of castes, etc. Such acts are contrary to what De Nobili calls the standard of righteousness. Cf. *Kantam* I, 46 -50.
[40] *Kantam*, II, 197-198.
[41] *Kantam*, I, 73.
[42] This is about *lilas*, or 'sport,' which are characteristics of certain gods in Hinduism. In *Kadavul Nirnayam*, De Nobili compares the true nature of God to what is found in Hinduism.

In his catechism called *Gnanopadesa Kurippidam*, De Nobili offers five tests by which one may distinguish between true and false religions: Does the God in it have all the attributes of a true God? Does it prohibit sins? Does it teach virtues and not vices? Is it consistent with human reason? Does it offer forgiveness of sins?[43] Such clear distinctions are crucial to the proclamation of the Gospel in a country where an astrophysicist and an astrologer have common ground in religion.

There are also qualitative differences between the God-languages of Hinduism and Christianity. Hindu notions of God are inadequate, for they stem from ignorance. Consider the following attributes of God in De Nobili's theological writings: God is spirit and is the cause of all effects. God possesses no body, lest he be limited and, therefore, will not be God. God is the Supreme Being (*Sarvesaran*) and the ruler over the whole world. God is eternal because he is self-existent and not created. God is perfect because he has no limitations, and God is all-wise and all-powerful. God is neither male nor female, nor animal nor tree, because He is the first and eminent cause. God is omnipresent by his knowledge, power, and causality. All creatures receive their life from God.

The writers of Hindu scriptures described God without any claim to revealed knowledge of God; they spoke of God as if He were an earthly king.[44] Such notions are imprecise and unclear. However, De Nobili was aware of the inadequacy of human language to express divine attributes completely. All humans, according to him, need a true knowledge of the person and work of God, which is essential for salvation. Only revealed religion offers such true and sufficient knowledge.

Salvation of Non-Christians

There are two kinds of religion in the teachings of De Nobili. Whereas the first one is limited to external rituals and ceremonies, the second addresses internal aspects of the human soul, such as knowing, loving, and serving God. The latter is the only legitimate way to salvation. A distinction exists between personal knowledge of God and a mere performance of religious ceremonies.[45] One cannot be saved through

---

[43] Cf., D. Yesudhas, "Indigenization or Adaptation?: A Brief Study of Roberto De Nobili's Attitude to Hinduism," *Bangalore Theological Forum*, I (1967): 39-52.
[44] *Kantam* (Doctrines), II, 193-95.
[45] This was one of the questions that the Brahmins' Court in Madurai raised at the trial of De Nobili. See Cronin, *Pearl*, 100, 101.

external ceremonies, such as bathing in the Ganges or frequenting the temples. Such notions come from human imagination.

De Nobili's theological dialogue with the Brahmins, in which he engaged doctrines such as the triune God, the incarnation of God, and the redemptive sufferings of Christ, was well known. He writes:

- With those who come to speak with me, I discuss no other questions than those which concern the salvation of their souls. In this matter.
- I treat of the existence of God and His attributes, how He is One and Three, how He created the world and men, and all other things.
- In addition, I teach how that very same God became man to save men. I declare that His name is Jesus Christ, which means Saviour, that He is true God and true Man, full of grace and divine gifts, who delivers us from sin, satisfies for the transgression of all men and offers a remedy against their errors.[46]

He has written about the question of the salvation of the non-Christian somewhat clearly.[47] According to him, there is a good non-Christian and a non-Christian who has not led a good life. The former belongs to a non-Christian religion and leads a morally good life. This morally good, religious person has several qualifications, such as rejecting false ideas about God in one's own religion and believing there is but one true God. He performs virtuous deeds,[48] but he has no knowledge of Christianity, the true religion of God.

The knowledge of God, which is not above the nature of human intellect, comes by the help of reason. Therefore, the love of God borne of this knowledge has a proportionate relation to the nature of the will of the person. This means that the virtues in this person are not meritorious unto salvation, but this does not mean that these virtues are realized without the grace of God. It means that salvation is a gift of God and that virtuous conduct is the way to the fulfillment of His salvific will.[49]

The knowledge, love and the virtuous deeds of a non-Christian can prevent him or her from committing serious sins, but they cannot be the

---

[46] Quoted by Cronin, 137.
[47] See *Dushana Dhikkaram* where he uses the works of St. Thomas Aquinas.
[48] Ibid., 413-414. Cf. Arokiasamy, 316.
[49] *Kantam II*, 294 - 295.

direct cause of salvation.⁵⁰ Although not supernatural, they are not done without God's grace.⁵¹ They prepare the good non-Christian for the grace of justification. The effect of sin in the non-Christian does not destroy natural reason; there is still some knowledge of truth by which one is able to perform deeds that are generally good.⁵²

In De Nobili's understanding, condemnation of the good non-Christian is not in keeping with the mercy of God.⁵³ He argues that it would be a disorder to condemn a good non-Christian who, through no fault of his own, did not know the Gospel of Christ. In such cases, God would send an earthly messenger or one from heaven to teach such a person the truth needed for salvation.⁵⁴ If such a person hears the truth and does not accept it, he or she will not be saved. But if the truth of salvation is accepted, then such a person can be saved.

The good deeds of the non-Christian prepare him or her to receive the saving grace, but they do not merit salvation. In *Atma Nirnayam*, he says that God who has willed to save people continually gives them the graces as good desires to do *dharma* and avoid sin.⁵⁵ Salvation is a supernatural gift. Therefore, it can never be produced by good human deeds of any individual.

The second category of non-Christian, according to De Nobili's definition, follows the non-Christian religion and has committed many sins. What should this person do to receive God's grace and hear the Gospel? The answer: reject sin and repent of the past, recognize God to be the Creator, and strive for salvation. One should do this because God is merciful and His salvific will is universal. This person can get help from his or her own religion to avoid errors about belief in God as well as in the practice of virtue.⁵⁶

---

⁵⁰ *Dushana Dhikkaram*, 415. Cf. Arokiasamy, 317.
⁵¹ De Nobili distinguishes between the external and internal graces (actual graces) which God bestows on all people and which is seen in such dispositions as fear of eternal punishment, desire to live according to God's will and the aversion of will to sin. Cf. De Nobili, *Atma Nirnayam* (Science of the Soul), p. 467.
⁵² Ibid.
⁵³ *Dushana Dhikkaram*, 435-436. Cf. Arokiasamy, 317.
⁵⁴ Arokiasamy, 317.
⁵⁵ *Atma Nirnayam*, 86, 92-93; Also *Dushana Dhikkaram*, 435-36. Cf. *Summa Theologica* I, 2, Q.112, a.3. Here, Aquinas teaches that a person's preparation for grace is from God, who is the Mover.
⁵⁶ Arokiasamy, 321. Cf. *Dushana Dhikkaram*, 433, 304, 305.

Concluding Critical Comments

The life and mission of Roberto De Nobili offer important lessons for cross-cultural missionaries:

First, his intellectual and theological preparation enabled him to understand the beliefs and practices of an ancient religious people. Missionaries should have adequate knowledge of the people and their scriptures to make their preaching effective. If properly investigated, one would find in these religions important linguistic tools that could be used in the contextualization of the Gospel.

Second, De Nobili's mastery of Sanskrit and other major languages enabled him to expound weighty theological matters with clarity and ease. The importance of Sanskrit for Indo-European languages is hardly understood by most students and teachers in colleges and seminaries in Western countries. As the standard of education declines in America, there is little hope that American seminaries can offer the kind of linguistic preparation that is essential to in-depth knowledge of Hinduism and other religions originated in India.

Third, his admiration of Indian culture, despite its complexity and seeming contradictions, is commendable. He dealt with deep-seated social attitudes and philosophies of the Brahmins. By identifying himself with the Brahmins, he entered into the inner world of the most orthodox Hindus of the time. Through cultural and linguistic expertise, he opened a fresh way for future missionaries to understand Hinduism from its original sources. Without such linguistic sources, one cannot teach Indian religions with all the seriousness that they demand. The study of foreign religions is still underdeveloped in American theological education.

Fourth, he was a great theologian, who showed remarkable openness to Hinduism. Nonetheless, he found no difficulty in rejecting its beliefs and claims that were inconsistent with his Christian faith. He brought clarity to the concepts and attributes of God, and he was deeply engaged in dialogue with the Brahmins. This interchange brought mutual understanding and increased clarity of both religions.

De Nobili was not a cultural imperialist who came with the notion of European superiority over Indian culture.[57] The church's missionary endeavors must be characterized by love and humility for the people. Such was not the attitude of many Western missionaries who went to

---

[57] Western missionaries have always believed in the superiority of their culture over the host culture in which they worked. See Stephen Neill, *Op. Cit.*, pp. 415- 416.

India. The words of Pathak are particularly relevant to the point we are making here:

> The missionaries who came to India in the first half of the Nineteenth century openly declared India to be a benighted land which could be raised only through the message of the Gospel. The missionary literature of this period is full of references to the spiritual misery of the people of India.... This attitude stemmed from the belief of early missionaries in their cultural superiority and the uniqueness of their spiritual message.[58]

The presence of a strong biblical and theological framework at the root of the Christian mission is another lesson one can learn from De Nobili. As a modern missionary to South India points out, one must insist on the primacy of the Holy Spirit, the need for genuine spirituality in the lives of the missionaries, and the positive outlook on the human knowledge and its important role in the proclamation of the Gospel.[59]

Today, a large number of Hindus from India has emigrated to the West.[60] Their growing significance raises questions about the need for a new kind of dialogue between Christianity and Hinduism. This includes equipping the churches and the seminaries for both understanding and dealing with the religious pluralism in the West.

---

[58] S. M. Pathak, *American Missionaries and Hinduism: A Study of Their Contacts from 1813 to 1910* (Delhi: Oriental Publishers, 1967), 78.

[59] Lesslie Newbigin's three foundational principles cited in Louis Luzbetak, *The Church and Cultures: New Perspectives in Missiological Anthropology* (Maryknoll, New York: Orbis Books, 1988), 1.

[60] An estimated 9 million Hindus live outside India with their own sets of beliefs and practices. For a cultural analysis of this transnational community, see Steven Vertovec, *The Hindu Diaspora: Comparative Patterns* (London and New York: Rutledge, 2000).

BIBLIOGRAPHY

Works of Roberto De Nobili in Tamil with translations available at De Nobili Research Institute, Tirunelveli, India. The following primary sources are important for those who work in this area of research.

Primary Sources – Selected
Roberto De Nobili's Original Writings in Tamil

Adaptation. Rajamanickam, S., ed., Tirunelveli: De Nobili Research Institute, 1971.
Indian Customs. Rajamanickam, S., ed., Tirunelveli: De Nobili Research Institute, 1972.
Gnanopadesam (Spiritual Teaching). It has five parts, and each part is called *kantam.*
Atma Nirnayam (Disquisition on the Soul), printed in Madras, 1889.
Agnana Nivaranam (Dispelling of Ignorance), printed in Trichinopoly, 1891.
Tivviya Madirigai (The Divine Model), printed in Pondicherry, 1870.
Punar Jenma Aksheba (Refutation of Rebirth). This is also known as *Nittiya Jivana Sallabam* (Dialogue on Eternal Life).
Dushana Dhikkaram (Refutation of blasphemies) Data unavailable
Gnana Sanchivi (Spiritual medicine) Data unavailable

Secondary Sources

Amaladass, Anand. *Jesuit Presence in Indian History*, Anand, Gujerat: Gujerat Sahitya Prakash, 1988.
Aquinas, Thomas. *Summa Theologica,* vols. II & III, Trans. Fathers of the English Dominican Province, Westminster, Maryland: Christian Classics, 1948.
Arokiasamy, Soosai. *Dharma, Hindu and Christian, According to Roberto De Nobili,* Roma: Editrice Pontificia Universita Gregoriana, 1986.
Bachmann, P. R. *Roberto De Nobili (1577-1656): Ein missionsgeschichtlicher Beitrag Zum Christlichen Dialog mit Hinduismus.* Rome: Bibliotheca Instituti Historici S.I. 32, Rome, 1972.
Cronin, Vincent. *A Pearl to India: The Life of Roberto De Nobili*, London: Rupert Hart-Davis, 1959.
Cross, F. L. & E. A. Livingstone, eds, *Oxford Dictionary of the Christian Church,* 2nd ed., London: Oxford University Press, 1974.
Gispert-Sauch, G., ed, *God's Word Among Men,* New Delhi: Vidyajyoti Institute of Religious Studies, 1973.
Lonergan, Bernard J. *Method in Theology*, Toronto: University of Toronto Press, 1971.
Luzbetak, Louis J. *The Church and Cultures: New Perspectives in Missiological Anthropology*, New York: Orbis Books, 1988.

Mahadevan, T. M. P. *Upanishads*, New Delhi: Arnold Heinemann Publishers, 1975.
Neill, Stephen. *Colonialism and Christian Missions*, London: Lutterworth Press, 1966.
Nida, Eugene and William Reyburn. *Meaning Across Cultures*, New York: Orbis Books, 1981.
Organ, Troy. *The Hindu Quest for the Perfection of Man*, Ohio: Ohio University Press, 1970.
Panikkar, K. M. *Asia and Western Dominance*, London: George Allen & Unwin, 1959.
Pathak, Sushil M. *American Missionaries and Hinduism*, New Delhi: Oriental Publishers, 1967.
Radhakrishnan, S. *The Principal Upanishads*, London: George Allen & Unwin, 1953.
Rahner, Karl. "Towards a Fundamental Theological Interpretation of Vatican II," *Theological Studies*, Vol. 40, Washington, D.C.: Georgetown University, 1977.
Rajamanickam, S. *The First Oriental Scholar*. Tirunelveli: De Nobili Research Institute, St. Xavier's College, 1972.
Sanneh, Lamin. *Translating the Message: The Missionary Impact on Culture*, Maryknoll, New York: Orbis Books, 1989.
Thomas, Joe M. "The Notion of *Communications* in the Theological Method of Bernard Lonergan," *Mission Today: A Journal of Missiological and Ecumenical Research*, Vol. V (Jan – March 2003).
Vertovec, Steven. *The Hindu Diaspora: Comparative Patterns*, London and New York: Rutledge, 2000.
Yesudhas, D. "Indigenization or Adaptation: A Brief Study of Roberto De Nobili's Attitude to Hinduism," *Bangalore Theological Forum* I (1967).

Chapter Three

Herman Dooyeweerd

Sphere Sovereignty and Modality: A Conceptual Introduction

Herman Dooyeweerd (1894-1977) was a Dutch legal philosopher whose writings are said to have contributed to a general renewal in philosophy in his days. He also is considered the most original philosopher that Holland has ever produced. His philosophy took its shape in the Reformed theology tradition. Dooyeweerd's writings are not widely known and read in other parts of the world, except through the works of groups of philosophers and theologians. The following words were written to provide the reader with an introduction to the thought of a great Christian thinker.

The best way to do this is to choose two of the fundamental concepts from Dooyeweerd's writings, namely, *Sphere Sovereignty* and *Modality* and discuss their importance in his thought. This approach would also lead us to make references to the question of autonomy in philosophical inquiry, which would, at least, open a window to the intellectual world of Dooyeweerd.

Dooyeweerd was a prolific writer who published some 200 books and articles. Although most of his works were in the fields of law and political theory, he wrote in other fields as well: ontology, epistemology, social philosophy, philosophy of science, aesthetics, philosophy of religion, and theology. Through writings and critical dialogue with contemporary philosophies, he was able to challenge what is called the "pretended autonomy" of theoretical thought in Western philosophy. He rejected the absolutization of human reason that played a major role in the presuppositions of such autonomy.

After completing studies at the Free University of Amsterdam, Dooyeweerd was appointed to various positions in the public sphere, including the assistant directorship of Kuyper Institute in The Hague. The Institute was a newly established research center of the

Antirevolutionary Party, one of the two major contemporary Christian political parties in the Netherlands. His positions gave him plenty of opportunities for reflection on the nature and task of Christian politics in the country. In 1926, Dooyeweerd was appointed to the chair of legal philosophy at the Free University of Amsterdam. He drew much of his inspiration from the tradition of Dutch Calvinism, as developed by Abraham Kuyper and other thinkers in the 19th century.

From his early days, Dooyeweerd was deeply interested in philosophy. Of all his writings, the four-volume work *A New Critique of Theoretical Thought*[156] (1953-58) is the magnum opus. He was a critic of Western thought (transcendental criticism), which he challenged from a Christian standpoint. Most importantly, he subjected Western philosophy to a complete scrutiny by asking the pertinent question, "Why is it, if philosophy is based on reason, the various schools of philosophy can never agree with each other?" He answers his own question by stating that it is because of their differing religious commitments, rather than the claims of unbiased reason, that cause disagreements among philosophers.

Dooyeweerd went on to establish through his writings a unified view of the world. To do so, he constructed a system of hierarchically ordered and inter-related realms of spheres, which are foundational to all created reality and which exist in an increasingly complex structural framework.

It is important to identify here the four religious ground motives (*grondmotief*, Dutch) in the historical development of Western philosophy, namely, form and matter in Greek philosophy, nature and grace in medieval culture, freedom and nature in modern humanism, and creation-fall-redemption in biblical philosophy. Dooyeweerd uses the biblical motive as an indispensible framework to evaluate all other motives and all philosophies arising from them. The biblical motive is both integral (embraces all things) and radical (penetrates to the root of created reality).[157] The Christian ground motive stands in radical antithesis to all other ground motives. He uses the term 'antithesis' to refer to the radical spiritual opposition that exists between the Kingdom of God and the kingdom of darkness.[158] This opposition exists in every

---

[156] *A New Critique of Theoretical Thought* (Lewiston, NY: Edwin Mellen Press), 1997. The words *critique* and *criticism* used here are not about the destruction of thought, but rather a delimiting of theoretical thought that marks the boundaries of theory.
[157] *Roots of Western Culture: Pagan, Secular, and Christian Options*, trans. John Kraay (Toronto: Wedge, 1979), p. 28.
[158] "For what the flesh desires is opposed to the Spirit, and what the Spirit desires

sphere of human life, including philosophy and academic activity as a whole. The Christian believer experiences this opposition in trying to live a life of undivided attention to God. The apostate religious motives have a false notion of god arising from the deification of some aspect of the creation. Such motives neither acknowledge nor honor the God of Christianity who is the Creator of heaven and earth.[159]

Embracing a biblical vision of the world, Dooyeweerd affirmed that reality is God's creation, called into existence by God and subjected to a temporal order that guarantees its coherence. Therefore, the very existence of our world carries and expresses meaning that is ordained by God.

In this respect, scholars view Dooyeweerd's entire work as an empirical effort to understand the character of our world by means of the insights derived from the Christian religion. The Christian insights that he used in articulating a philosophy were not something added to his thought later on but an integral part of it. The biblical ground motive of creation-fall-redemption is seen as a driving force in the religious root of this temporal life. He argues that a person who has been gripped by this motive is to have a "radical conversion of his life's stance and of his whole view of temporal life."[160]

There exists an intrinsic link between religion and the whole of life, a link that often is stressed in Reformed theology. The discovery of this link is vital to the task of doing philosophy responsibly. This is why the creation-fall-redemption motive is both essential and non-negotiable for Dooyeweerd, because it provides him with keys for interpreting the patterns of history and culture. The ground motive is a spiritual driving force that can inspire all understanding, interpretation, and actions. The human heart is religious in nature, and the ground motive governs all of life's temporal expressions from this religious center of life (Proverbs 4:23: "Keep your heart with all diligence, for out of it are the issues of life").

According to Dooyeweerd, a spirit is directly operative in the religious ground motive, which is either the spirit of God or that of an idol.[161] In this case, the individual does not control the spirit, but the spirit controls the individual. The point of departure in all our academic or intellectual

---

is opposed to the flesh; for these are opposed to each other, to prevent you from doing what you want" (Gal. 5:17).
[159] *Roots*, 29.
[160] Ibid., 40.
[161] Ibid., 9.

investigation is the religious ground motive. For example, scientific activity one carries out is not a neutral activity with respect to religion.[162]

Dooyeweerd identifies several religious ground motives (*religieuze grondmotieven*) in the cultural and spiritual development of the West. The most important of these are the spirit of ancient civilizations (Greece and Rome), Christendom, and modern humanism. These are apostate motives. Over the years, these ground motives have at various times gained the upper hand in the historic process in the West.

The relation between theology and philosophy in Dooyeweerdian thought is well established. He explores this relationship especially in one of his lectures,[163] starting with St. Augustine and proceeding to St. Thomas to Karl Barth, explaining what each one thought of this relationship. For Dooyeweerd, the knowledge of God and of self that arises from the Word-revelation (written revelation) is of great importance in both philosophy and theology. One cannot do theology without this scriptural ground motive; neither can one do philosophy in the true sense of the word. The revelation of God in Jesus Christ and the religious demands it makes upon human life should serve as the starting point of philosophy, and only such a "radically Christian philosophy" can serve as the foundation for a Christian theology.[164] Dooyeweerd's intellectual world was closely linked to that of Abraham Kuyper. Reared in the neo-Calvinistic culture, Dooyeweerd studied at the Free University and earned his doctorate there in 1917.

Dooyeweerd in Relation to Kuyper

Abraham Kuyper (1837-1920) was a theologian and statesman who became prime minister of the Netherlands in 1900. He is also remembered for his development of the doctrine of "common grace." In 1880, he established the Free University of Amsterdam, becoming its first head and the most prominent professor from the time of its founding to the time he became the prime minister of the country in 1901. The concept of *Sphere Sovereignty*, one of the subjects of our discussion, was first stated by Kuyper. He opened the Free University of Amsterdam with an address on Sphere Sovereignty, a social and political theory he had developed as an intellectual justification to create structural means of

---

[162] Ibid.
[163] See *In the Twilight of Western Thought: Studies in the Pretended Autonomy of Philosophical Thought* (Lewiston: New York, 1999), 79.
[164] Ibid., 104.

limiting the power of the state. The state must not interfere with the working of the academy.

Kuyper's influence permeated Dooyeweerd's life, especially in the five areas of the principle of the sovereignty of God as the basic idea of philosophy, the grounding of all human thought and science in the heart, the doctrine of common grace as the foundation of human culture, the doctrine of the antithesis between regenerated and unregenerated human science, and his doctrine of sphere sovereignty.[165]

The Calvinistic world and life-view created a religiocultural movement in the Netherlands, and Dooyeweerd lived in that particular intellectual milieu. Kuyper saw Calvinism not as merely a theology but as a complete view of all of life and the world, with direct implications for every area of human experience. This view was deeply rooted in the Bible. Dooyeweerd spent much of his time propagating and working out the basic biblical worldview taught by Abraham Kuyper.

Dooyeweerd followed Kuyper in his understanding of sphere sovereignty. He also added to it what is known as "the fifteen modal aspects," emphasizing particularly their irreducibility, which will be explained later in this chapter.

Sphere Sovereignty/Universality and Modality

Sphere Sovereignty (*soevereiniteit in eigen kring*)

In 1816, King William I issued a decree imposing on the Dutch Reformed Church the 'General Regulations" regarding the administration of the church. Apparently the King did not realize that he had far exceeded his legal competence. He did not know that such regulations would be contradictory to the essential nature and the laws of the church.[166]

Another incident occurred in the 1930s when the Dutch government forbade housewives from making butter from cheap ingredients. The housewives complained: "Am I no longer boss in my own kitchen?"

The intrusion of the government into the private life of its people has become more pervasive and scandalous in our own day. Audio, video, photographs, e-mails, documents, and connection logs are collected in order to enable analysts to track a person's movements and contacts over time. It is said that they can watch your ideas form as you type.

---

[165] "Kuyper's Wetenschapsleer," *Philosophia Reformata*, 4 (1939): 193-232.
[166] This and the following example are from L. Kalsbeek, *Contours of Christian Philosophy* (Toronto: Wedge, 1975), 91.

Obviously, the two spheres are in conflict with each other in both examples cited above. The point is that one sphere must not usurp the authority of the other. Each has its own God-ordained norms that are in operation.

Kuyper presented sphere sovereignty as a creational principle to refer to the various, distinct spheres of human authority, such as family, school, church, and industry. Each sphere has its own responsibility and decision-making power, which may not be usurped by those in authority in another sphere. Accordingly, there is an authority that is proper to each domain and that is to be rightly exercised by its leader in direct responsibility to God. Kuyper's dynamic vision of Sphere Sovereignty under Christ had formative influences upon Dooyeweerd.

Dooyeweerd continued his work with Kuyper's vision, which stated that God, the absolute sovereign, has given each sphere in human society its own particular laws of life by which it should live. So, the spheres mentioned above have their own sovereignty. Each sphere derives its authority, not from the state, but from God. Therefore, they are accountable to God alone, and not to the state. Each sphere functions in accordance with its inner nature and strictly within its jurisdiction. Kuyper stated in his address to the Free University that without sphere sovereignty, the state would have unlimited power to transgress the boundaries of the sphere which the Creator has set for it.

Dooyeweerd retains the term *sphere sovereignty*, which is the ontological principle on which the sociological principle is based, as each of the societal "spheres" is qualified by a different irreducible modality. The idea of modality (or modal aspect) is an important contribution of Dooyeweerd which we shall explain a little later.

Sphere Universality

The concept of "sphere universality" is the counterpart of sphere sovereignty. In this respect, all the modalities (aspects) are intimately connected with each other in an unbreakable coherence. Whereas sphere sovereignty stresses the unique distinctiveness and irreducibility of the modal aspects, sphere universality emphasizes the fact that every modal aspect depends for its meaning on all others.

Modality

Human beings experience the world in a multiplicity of modes or ways. Modality is one of the fifteen *fundamental ways of being* distinguished by

Dooyeweerd. Some synonyms for modality are A*spect, Function, Law-Sphere,* and *Meaning-Side.* Also used was the Latin *Modus Quo* (manner in which) to stress the fact that a modality is a *manner* or *way* in which a thing exists or functions, and not something in and of itself. They pertain to a mode or a *way of being.* The following are the fifteen modalities (or aspects) that Dooyeweerd names:[167]

1. Numerical/Arithmetic (Has a numerical aspect, a number side).
2. Spatial (Needs space to occupy)
3. Kinematic (Moves or contains movement)
4. Physical (Has a physical aspect)
5. Biotic (Pertains to breathing, circulation, digestion, etc.)
6. Sensitive (Pertains to psychological aspect)
7. Analytic (Has ability to analyze; could be subject of analysis)
8. Historical (Has a historical aspect)
9. Lingual (Develops systems of symbols and language)
10. Social (Has social cohesion and relationship with others in society)
11. Economic (Pertains to financial aspect)
12. Aesthetic (Has aspect of beauty and art)
13. Juridical (Pertains to legal aspect)
14. Ethical (Pertains to moral aspect)
15. Pistic/Faith (Has a faith aspect; one of the most fundamental ways of being religious)

Everything in temporal reality, according to Dooyeweerd's view, displays these aspects or modalities. For example, the Church can be described as having all these modal aspects. The created reality has a "religious root unity" and the modalities are present in it. It is like light refracts into the hues of the rainbow when it passes through the prism and displays the colors.

---

[167] *Kinematic* was a later addition to the original list. One could take any created reality to examine these aspects, for example, a plant, having a numerical aspect (with certain number of petals or leaves), spatial aspect (which needs space to occupy, etc.), and so on.

Dooyeweerd consistently emphasizes the unity and coherence of God's creation. The modalities he suggests may be investigated by the special sciences, such as mathematics, physics, chemistry, biology, psychology, logic, history, linguistics, sociology, economics, aesthetics, legal theory, ethics, theology, and so on. Each of these sciences considers reality in only one of its aspects.[168]

If a physicist is investigating the distinct aspect of his/her sphere (physics), he/she should do so in relation to the rest of the spheres. Each modal aspect answers to its own peculiar law that governs it. If the physicist is investigating these distinct aspects without the light of God's knowledge in his/her heart, he/she would be like the person who sees the colors of the rainbow but is not aware of the unbroken light from which they arise.[169] Each color must be seen in relation to all other colors, instead of objectifying and absolutizing whatever color appeals to him/her the most. Dooyeweerd warns against abstracting, objectifying, and absolutizing one aspect of the created reality over against all other aspects. There exists an indissoluble coherence among all modalities, and if any one modality is abstracted from the others to become the explanation for the rest, this coherence is broken and the created reality loses the wholeness of its meaning.

In other words, one must not present one aspect of reality as reality in its completeness. This would lead one to reductionism, which is reducing something to something else to give a theoretical explanation of it in other terms. Dooyeweerd opposes the many forms of reductionism, which does not recognize the richness and diversity of God's creation. Therefore, it is important to stress in any intellectual investigation the irreducibility and sphere sovereignty of each reality.

Significance of Dooyeweerd's Work

The Use of Christian Ground Motive

Dooyeweerd appears to be the only philosopher who was nurtured in a Christian community and who challenged the philosophical methods of his day while remaining loyal to his Christian roots. The value of his work lies in the foundation he establishes for future scholars by employing the biblical ground motive for doing philosophy.

---

[168] *Roots of Western Culture: Pagan, Secular, and Christian Options,* trans. John Kraay (Toronto: Wedge Publishing, 1979), 41.
[169] Ibid.

As opposed to all other ground motives that lay hidden in philosophy, Christian religious ground motive has its foundation in Scriptures. It upholds the biblical understanding of God, the fall of humanity due to sin, and the redemption through Christ in communion with the Holy Spirit. He rightly argues that the whole temporal world has its root unity in the humanity's religious community. The human fall into sin and estrangement from God resulted in the fall of all creation, because the meaning and purpose of creation were intrinsically linked to humanity.[170] What befalls humanity will affect the created world in which it is placed.

Rejection of Philosophy that Begins in the Sphere of Creation

Dooyeweerd rejects immanence philosophy, which views philosophy as self-sufficient. This self-sufficiency is not possible because there exists a religious ground motive in the formulation of any philosophy. Immanence philosophy is rooted in the creation, and as such, it cannot transcend the boundary of the creation. As a result, immanent-holding philosophers run into the problem of absolutizing some features or aspects of creation itself. This reductionism is what happened in Western philosophy. Therefore, he strongly argues that philosophy as a pure rational thinking is free of religious beliefs – either theistic or atheistic – cannot exist.

Unmasking the False Claims of Objective, Autonomous Human Reason

Dooyeweerd is a critic of presuppositions used in Western philosophy. He lays a strong foundation for Christian thinkers in their own examination of modern philosophy. He believes that the need for Christian faith commitment in philosophical thought is essential for such a critical activity. As stated at the outset, he rejects the pretended autonomy of European philosophers. The idea of "pure reason" which many philosophers claimed for their work, is impossible. Therefore, Dooyeweerd calls on Christian philosophers to engage in self-critique as well as in development of an integral Christian philosophy that has a strong biblical foundation. One must understand the "primordial role of faith in theory formation," and any insistence on "the pretended autonomy of theoretical thought is an illusion."[171]

---

[170] *Roots*, 31.
[171] James H. Olthius, "Love/Knowledge: Sojourning with Others, Meeting with Differences," *Knowing Other-wise: Philosophy at the Threshold of Spirituality*, James

The pretended autonomy that Dooyeweerd criticizes in Western philosophy is a point well taken. All theoretical thought and intellectual inquiry start with 'pre-theoretical' or 'supra-theoretical' commitments that function as the condition of the possibility of theory. The claim of philosophers that they need only some objective reason as starting-point for philosophy is to be dismissed. The commitments that serve as a starting point have an ultimate nature and are indicative of "innate religious impulse of the ego." There is a hidden role of religious motive – either in the direction of God or in the direction of apostasy. The genuine dialogues among philosophers cannot happen until the hidden motives are exposed.

Concluding Critical Comments: Secularization of the West and the Need for Re-evangelization

The claim of supposed autonomy requires further explanation and application. The Autonomous period in the West was from 1700 to 1900 A.D. and followed the collapse of the medieval culture and a period of transition. The Autonomous culture placed much stress on the human mind and its power to reason, which was a radical departure from the church-centered medieval worldview. The church was no longer considered the sole dispenser of grace and truth. Instead, the Autonomous culture sought no revelation from God or help from the church. When scientists and scholars began to depend on their own reason and empirical observation, a new understanding of the world, which was antithetical to the medieval biblical worldview, emerged.

The Autonomous culture rejected divine revelation and tradition as universal primary sources for truth. Instead, the language of natural science was accepted as the language of truth. As a result, problems were reduced to mathematical formulae (reductionism). This concept, along with other intellectual forces, eventually led to the secularization of the West and, in general, excluded all assumptions about God. This new approach became the new way of thinking in the modern world.

The process of secularization in the West was gradual and was clearly pronounced in the fields of human knowledge from astronomy and physics to biology, history, sociology, and psychology. This process enabled scholars and scientists to explain the material world without reference to God's revelation. For example, historian David Hume (1711-

---

H. Olthius, ed. (Bronx, NY: Fordham University Press, 1997), 12-13.

1776) argued that miracles cannot happen because they lie outside the Autonomous Person's philosophy of history.[172]

Likewise, Edward Gibbon argued[173] in *The Decline and Fall of the Roman Empire* that God had not caused the fall of the Roman Empire as a punishment for evil and that, instead, it was the result of a series of particular natural historical events.

Interestingly, this new approach to human knowledge was applied also to the study of the sacred Scriptures. The Biblical texts began to be investigated and reinterpreted from a naturalistic perspective, quite different from what the church had held.

The Autonomous worldview and its modern scientific methodology have made a serious impact upon the culture. At least in part, this approach brought Europe into a state of apostasy, where the church is marginalized and the divine revelation is banished from the human sciences, rendering the West one of the most needy mission fields.

Dooyeweerd believes that Christians will be able to exert a specifically Christian influence in the fields of law, politics, education, labor relations and industry only if they can put forward truly Christian answers to the many problems of the society. Furthermore, the answers are available to Christians if they will make the necessary effort and will submit their minds and hearts to God's Word and be guided by the Holy Spirit.

---

[172] John F. Wilson and W. Royce Clark, *Religion: A Preface*, 2nd ed. (Englewood Cliffs, NJ: Prentice Hall, 1989, 1982), 144, 145.

[173] See the abbreviated version in Dero A. Saunders, ed. *The Portable Gibbon: The Decline and fall of the Roman Empire* (New York: Viking, 1952).

BIBLIOGRAPHY

Dooyeweerd, Herman. *Roots of Western Culture: Pagan, Secular, and Christian Options*. Trans. John Kraay. Toronto: Wedge, 1979.
-----*In the Twilight of Western Thought*, Lewiston, NY: The Edwin Mellen Press, 1999.
-----*A New Critique of Theoretical Thought*, 4 vols, Philadelphia: P&R Publications, 1953-58. Reprint, St. Catherine: Paideia, 1983.
Kuyper, Abraham. *Lectures on Calvinism*, Grand Rapids: Eerdmans, 1931.
McIntire, C. Thomas, ed., *The Legacy of Herman Dooyeweerd*, Lanham, MD: The University Press of America, 1985.
Kalsbeek, L. *Contours of a Christian Philosophy: An Introduction to Herman Dooyeweerd's Thought*, Toronto: Wedge Publishing Foundation, 1975.
Taylor, Hebden E.L. *The Christian Philosophy of Law, Politics, and the State*, Nutley, NJ: The Craig Press, 1966.
Wilson, John F. & W. Royce Clark. *Religion: A Preface*, 2nd ed., Englewood Cliffs, NJ: Prentice Hall, 1989, 1982.
Wolters, Albert. *Creation Regained*, Downers Grove, IL: IVP, 1985.

Chapter Four

Karl Rahner

Original Sin in the Light of the Human Situation

The sinful condition and state in which human beings are born is generally designated by the term *peccatum originale*, which is translated literally as *original sin*. The doctrine of original sin is among the most fundamental teachings of the Christian Church since the time of St. Augustine, in whose work this doctrine came to receive fuller theological attention. The doctrine became a subject of controversy with Pelagianism.[1] Since the time of Augustine, the Church has authoritatively taught the doctrine of original sin. As early as 418 A.D., the Council of Carthage upheld it, and later it received much attention from the Council of Trent. Karl Rahner (1904–1984) has given a new dimension to its interpretation, which is the subject of this chapter. Much of Rahner's explication of this dogma took place in the context of the Council of Trent. In his theological writings, the doctrine of original sin is placed closely to other related doctrines, such as `grace and nature,' the `supernatural existential,' and the `created order.'

The purpose of this chapter is to examine Rahner's understanding of the nature of original sin in the light of the human situation and to relate its significance to the life of the Church.

In order to better understand Rahner's view on the nature of original sin, one must recognize at the outset at least three reasons for calling it original sin. *First*, the sin is derived from the original root of the human

---

[1]Pelagianism denied all original sin. The phrases *propagatione, non-imitatione* that are used in the declaration of the Council of Trent with regard to the transmission of Adam's sin were intended to refute the Pelagian view that original sin is really personal sin committed in imitation of the sin of Adam. See also Chapter One of this work.

race. *Second*, it is present in the life of every individual from the time of birth, and, therefore, it cannot be regarded as the result of imitation. *Finally*, it is understood as the root of all actual sins that defile human life. The first man, Adam, was created in the image of God, and by virtue of this likeness, he was endowed with original justice, holiness, and sanctifying grace. Adam was given freedom from bodily and mental suffering as well as freedom from concupiscence. However, Adam's sin deprived him of sanctifying grace, and it brought about death and concupiscence, not only for him but for the whole human race.

Rahner's Interpretation of Original Sin

Rahner's interpretation of the doctrine of original sin reveals a trend that is both fresh and distinct. The dogma of original sin, according to Rahner, cannot be rationalistically disintegrated but must be taken into account seriously. Therefore, he favors an objective and epistemological approach as the basis of inquiry into this doctrine.[2] Thus, the starting point is neither the unintelligible imputation of Adam's sin nor the collective guilt incurred.[3] The discussion of original sin, according to Rahner, must begin with our own human situation, which, for us, is co-determined by the guilt of others. This approach is important for a proper understanding of the dogma.[4] In his view, the doctrine of original sin is a datum of the New Testament theology, and not in itself primary revelation. Our sinfulness is a sinfulness that has been derived.[5] In other words, Rahner is proposing what is called a "retrospective aetiology," which starts with what is known in a given situation.

The human situation, for an individual who is a free subject, is his presupposition for freedom. It is determined by history and by other people. One cannot escape it. It is prior to the human person. One's unique acts of freedom can take place only in this given situation, meaning that one's situation is conditioned by a permanent presence of guilt from an outside source. Rahner calls this condition a co-determination of an individual's situation by others' guilt. This co-determination is ineradicable and inescapable, and, therefore, it is a

---

[2] *Sacramentum Mundi*, IV, 330.
[3] Ibid.
[4] "Man as a Being Threatened Radically by Guilt," *Foundations of Christian Faith*, trans. William V. Dych (New York: The Crossroad Publishing Co., 1978), 111.
[5] "The Sin of Adam," *Theological Investigations*, XI, 249, 259, 262.

permanent feature of any individual's situation.[6] This guilt is already deposited in the origin of human history. Thus the individual person's nature already bears the mark of the guilt of others. This is an important strand in the situational interpretation of original sin.

An important consideration in the understanding of the human situation is the unity and interdependence of the human race visible in its spatiotemporal history.[7] Such a view of the integral nature of the human race aids in the retrospective method of looking at original sin and guilt. This is how Rahner expresses it:

> The universality and the ineradicable nature of the co-determination of the situation of freedom by guilt in the single history of the human race implies an original determination of this human situation by guilt already present at the beginning.[8]

However, Rahner does not believe that Adam's original act of freedom at the beginning of the single human history was transmitted to the succeeding generations in its moral quality. In other words, he does not favor the idea of a biological transmission of original sin, which is an essential element, for example, in the writings of several Reformation theologians.[9] The point of departure for a correct understanding of the knowledge, meaning, and experience of original sin is a religious-existential interpretation of our own situations.[10] Therefore, the first act of sin, namely, the sin of Adam, is not imputed to us. This is the reason:

> Personal guilt from an original act of freedom cannot be transmitted, for it is the existential no of personal transcendence towards God or against him. And by its very nature this cannot be transmitted, just as the formal freedom of a subject cannot be transmitted.[11]

---

[6] *Foundations*, 107.

[7] "The sin of Adam," 107.
[8] *Foundations*, 110.
[9] Ibid.
[10] Ibid.
[11] Ibid., 111.

Rahner adds a new hermeneutical dimension to the doctrine of original sin when he proposes two existentials[12] of every human situation, namely, sin and grace. These two existentials are described by Saint Paul in Romans 5:15-17:

> But the free gift is not like the trespass. For if the many died through the one man's trespass, much more surely have the grace of God and the free gift in the grace of the one man, Jesus Christ, abounded for the many. And the free gift is not like the effect of the one man's sin. For the judgment following one trespass brought condemnation, but the free gift following many trespasses brings justification. If, because of the one man's trespass, death exercised dominion through that one, much more surely will those who receive the abundance of grace and the free gift of righteousness exercise dominion in life through the one man, Jesus Christ.

These are two situations, one of disaster and the other of salvation. One is disastrous because of the sinful action of the first parents and its consequences for the entire human race. The other is the situation of salvation, because it comes from the redemptive work of Christ. Although Adam's sin occurred prior to the work of Christ, original sin is not ultimately prior in time of redemption.[13] Each individual ratifies, by his or her own free decision, either by faith in Jesus Christ or by personal sin, the situation of his or her own choice. In either of these existential considerations, the human situation is prior to personal decision. It is already there.

Rahner discusses the notion of infralapsarianism, which refers to God's foreknowledge of the sin of Adam that constituted his fall. God, whose saving power is greater than the power of sin, permitted sin within his overall design and desire to save all people. This saving will of God is a permanent existential. These two existential aspects, one of perdition and disaster and the other of redemption, are ever present with human

---

[12] The term was first used by Martin Heidegger to designate those components that were constitutive of human existence by which human beings were distinguished from other kinds of beings. See William V. Dych, *Karl Rahner* (Collegeville, MN.: Liturgical Press, 1992), 36.

[13] *Sacramentum Mundi*, IV, 329.

beings. Therefore, according to Rahner, the human situation in relation to salvation is dialectically determined [14] and may be nullified by an individual's decision either for perdition or for salvation. Now the question remains as to what happens to an existential against which the person has made the decision. The answer is that it is not suppressed because man always remains in the situation of concupiscence and death and in that of being redeemed.[15]

Original sin is a real and interior sin and can rightly be called man's situation. It is not something external to humanity or a human person, because, as he points out:

> It is part of this situation in which the free decision is made, whether for salvation or ruin, that because of Adam, grace is not at man's disposal as the content and means of the decision about salvation which is required of him.[16]

The most important element of the state of original sin is privation of sanctifying grace. In Rahner's thought, there is a situational lack of the divinizing *Pneuma* that is contrary to the will of God, and this lack means a state of guilt. God does not owe grace to anyone, but He offers it to human beings, not because they are in Adam but because of the redemptive work of Christ. This Rahner calls an infralapsarian ordination to Christ.[17]

The notion of the unity of the human race is used by Rahner to link our history to that of Adam. Although we are far removed from the origin of human history and the original act of sin, in our own situations, we are indeed the children of Adam because we stand in a physical and historical connection with the beginning of humanity. This connection with the beginning of humanity is vital to the explanation of the situational privation of the holy *Pneuma*. We are Adam's children, and we become guilty, but only in an analogous sense. The privation of holy grace antecedent to the free decision of the individual implies the nature of sin. It is a state in which ontological holiness is lacking. The mode of a

---

[14] Ibid., 334.
[15] Ibid.
[16] Ibid., 333.
[17] Ibid., 107.

human generation has no significance in the consideration of the dogma of original sin because humanity has the same origin, unity, and telos in God's economy.[18] A situational presence of grace and situational absence of grace, as Rahner describes, appear to be a contradiction. One needs to ask more questions about the intrinsic nature and the qualitative distinction of these two situations that Rahner describes.

Rahner's exposition is a situational reinterpretation of the dogma of original sin. Original sin is a situation in which we find ourselves. By means of aetiological method, original sin is derived from the sin of Adam. It is the historical origin of the present predicament.[19] This privation of grace is not the fault of those who are presently experiencing it as existential, but it was precipitated by the act of the first parents. It resulted from a fall at the origin of human history.

This way of interpreting original sin is seen as a new attempt at creating a theological appeal to the present-day individuals. This new approach makes the dogma more appealing to modern people.[20] Furthermore, the etiological method by which original sin is derived from the primordial fall is a new way of looking at this problem. However, this approach may be seen as negating the element of personal responsibility in original sin. As the situation is co-determined by the guilt of others, Rahner's position may give one occasion to complain about his situation. In Adam, we see not only the privation of sanctifying grace but also the presence of positive evil. The element of our personal responsibility in the sin of Adam is very clear. Moreover, it is held that original sin is also conveyed by natural generation. Accordingly, all descendants of Adam are conceived and born in sin (Psalm 51:5).

Rahner makes three observations about the three-fold misunderstanding of original sin.[21] *First*, it is seen as a contradiction to the present-day conception of human nature as good, sound, and whole. Although people may believe that there are defects in individual and social lives, they think these are "progressively eliminable." In this regard, original sin comes as a contradiction to the quest for a free and

---

[18] cf. "Monogenism," *Sacramentum Mundi*, IV, 106.
[19] *Foundations*, 114.
[20] George Vandervelde, *Original Sin: Two Major Trends in Roman Catholic Reinterpretation* (Washington, D.C: University Press of America, Inc., 1981), 256.
[21] *Sacramentum Mundi*, IV, 327.

fortunate human condition. *Second*, original sin is identical with the tragic nature of human existence as having finite existence. It does not stem from any primordial historical event at the beginning of human genesis; it is simply the constitutive nature of humans and it cannot be abolished.[22] *Third*, many misunderstand original sin as identical with personal sin. These beliefs about original sin are inconsistent with a biblical understanding of the doctrine.

Concluding Critical Comments

Rahner views the doctrine of original sin as a vital point to address the core of theology and human existence. He provides a new dimension through his masterful and distinctive exposition, which not only informs the mind of a scholar but also transforms his or her daily Christian living. His attempt at removing the prevailing misunderstanding about this doctrine is commendable. With full force and vigor, Rahner states that the doctrine of original sin and the serious reality that it entails are not some "sterile theological knowledge," used once in a while to teach as catechism truth.

According to Rahner, academic theology is not an end in itself. Rather, it is used in the service of the Church's faith and witness. His criticism of the lukewarm attitude of the Church toward the handling of this doctrine is well-founded. In following Rahner's admonition, we should ask ourselves the questions: Does the church, which has multiple forms of ministry, regard the doctrine of original sin seriously and teach about it in its spiritual formation? Does this doctrine play a major role in its presentation of Christianity to the non-Christian world? In conclusion, the need for emphasizing the reality and seriousness of original sin in the church's preaching and its dialog with members of non-Christian religions cannot be ignored.

---

[22] Ibid.

BIBLIOGRAPHY

Calvin, John. *Institutes of the Christian Religion*, Vol. I, John T. McNeil, ed, Philadelphia: The Westminster Press, 1940.

Dych, William V. *Karl Rahner*, Collegeville, MN. The Liturgical Press, 1992.

Pendergast, R.J., "The Supernatural Existential, Human Generation and Original Sin," *Downside Review*, LXXXII, Exeter: Catholic Records Press, 1964.

Rahner, Karl. *Foundations of Christian Faith: An Introduction to the Idea of Christianity*, Dych, William V. (ed), New York: Crossroad, 1987.

------*Sacramentum Mundi*, IV, Montreal: Palm Press, 1969.

------ (ed), *The Encyclopedia of Theology: The Concise Sacramentum Mundi*, New York: Crossroad, 1975.

------- "Original Sin, Polygenism and Freedom," *Theology Digest*, XXI, St. Louis: St. Louis University (St. Louis School of Divinity), 1973.

------*Theological Investigations*, XI, trans. David Bourke, London: Darton, Longman and Todd, 1974.

Vandervelde, George. *Original Sin: Two Major Trends in Roman Catholic Reinterpretation*, Washington D.C: University Press of America, 1981.

Chapter Five

Karl Barth

The Meaning of the Baptism of the Holy Spirit

The doctrine of the Baptism with the Holy Spirit has long been a subject of controversy among Christians. One of the Christian movements to sweep across continents has been Neo-Pentecostalism,[1] for which the Baptism with the Holy Spirit is a distinct doctrine. The phenomenal growth of the Assemblies of God and similar movements, which emphasize speaking in tongues as a sign of the Holy Spirit baptism, has been a matter of interest for theologians of all stripes.

Before we turn to the Karl Barth's thoughts on the subject, some observations are made about the Pentecostal churches. The traditional Pentecostal teaching[2] makes several claims, among them that:

• Jesus' disciples were born again before the Day of Pentecost but had to wait for the promised Spirit (Acts 1:4).

• Jesus told them that "before many days you shall be baptized with the Holy Spirit" (Acts 1:5), which was fulfilled on the Day of Pentecost. According to the promise of the Lord, "they were filled with the Holy Spirit and began to speak in other tongues, as the Spirit gave them utterance" (Acts 2:4).

These texts clearly show that the disciples received a baptism in (or with) the Holy Spirit. Although they were born again long before the Day of Pentecost, the Baptism with the Spirit has to be viewed as a subsequent experience of spiritual empowerment, accompanied by the gift of speaking in tongues. There are both Protestants and Roman Catholics who claim to have received the Baptism of the Holy Spirit and the gift of tongues. The

---

[1] Neo-Pentecostal movement gradually assumed the name "Charismatic." See Frederick D. Bruner, *A Theology of the Holy Spirit* (London: Hodder & Stoughton, 1970), 52, for a well-documented discussion of the history and theology of various Pentecostal groups.

[2] See Wayne Grudem, *Systematic Theology* (Grand Rapids: Zondervan, 1994), chapter 39, for a comprehensive presentation of the subject.

Baptism with the Holy Spirit is a New Testament teaching, and it has implications for the life of Christians.

With these preliminary observations, we turn to Karl Barth's teachings on the subject. The particular aim of this study is to understand Barth's idea of the Baptism with the Holy Spirit and its meaning for the believer's life. Such a study can be carried out best in the immediate context of his writing on the subject. In order to achieve this goal, I shall focus on the most direct treatment of the subject in his *Church Dogmatics, IV/4 (Fragment)*. References to other parts of his writing will also be made, so that a more balanced understanding of his teaching on the subject can be presented.

Barth's Doctrine of the Baptism of the Holy Spirit

Barth has not produced any work in the area of Pneumatology. His discussion of the Holy Spirit is dispersed throughout the many volumes of his *Church Dogmatics*. Therefore, one must explore different sections of *Church Dogmatics* in order to bring together various strands of discussions that deal with the Holy Spirit. These strands are not always set forth in a plain and indisputable form that yields a clear understanding of his theology of the Spirit's work in the Trinitarian context. For example, IV/1 contains a presentation of the nature and work of the Holy Spirit. As the awakening power of God, the Spirit is seen here as the one who gathers the Christian community. In IV/2, the Spirit is introduced in relation to the up-building of the Christian community. As these volumes were written over a period of time, they cannot be said to have an internally consistent discussion of the Holy Spirit. An extensive study that identifies and arranges the various strands existing within the rich pneumatological material, which is necessary for a full understanding of Barth's thought, is beyond the scope of this chapter. The major concern here is to understand what Barth thought about the doctrine of the Holy Spirit baptism in the context in which he discusses it.

Distinction Between Water Baptism and Spirit Baptism

There is a clear distinction in Barth's thought between water baptism and the baptism with the Holy Spirit. In the *Fragment*,[3] the former is treated as an outward attestation or confirmation of the latter, producing a spiritual correlation. In this teaching, water baptism is distinguished from the

---

[3] *Fragment*, 1-40.

baptism of the Spirit.[4] Whereas the former is the result of human decision, the latter is accomplished by God himself. Barth is clear about the purpose of these two baptisms. The human decision for water baptism does not merit any individual the Christian life, which can come only from Christ.[5] It is, rather, the "beginning of an obedient life."[6] The baptism with the Holy Spirit is the "divine preparation of man for the Christian life in its totality."[7] Both baptisms are essential for a faithful and obedient life before God.

Sharing of the History of Jesus

The Christian transformation, for Barth, is the result of the living connection one has to the history of Jesus Christ, in which the Christian has an actual share. The Baptism with the Holy Spirit is both fundamental and decisive in the salvation history of the Christian, and implies a decisive Christian change that is radical and transformative. Through that change, the person is set free to live a life of faithfulness to God. Accordingly, "it is the exaltation of our essence with all its possibilities and limits into the completely different sphere of that totality, freedom, correspondence and service."[8] It reveals not only the freedom of God but also the bestowal of the freedom upon the person by the Spirit of God. The change that is produced by the Holy Spirit Baptism is a creative one: it is the source of Christian life.

The pivotal point, for Barth, in the understanding of the Spirit Baptism and the ensuing change is the significance of the history of Jesus Christ, which is the cause of this change. This history, which is different from all other histories, serves as the strong foundation of the Christian life. The Christian's life has its origin in the knowledge and contents of the history of the Son of God. The change that the Christian undergoes at the Baptism of the Holy Spirit is both distinct and divine. It is distinct from all other changes and happenings, whether natural or supernatural. The change that is created by the Baptism of the Spirit is solely based on the history of Jesus, which has "awakening, quickening and enlightening" power.[9] Apart from a genuine change and a new, transformed vision, no one can be faithful to God. Therefore, it is the work of the Holy Spirit to facilitate this change,

---

[4] Ibid., 30, 31.
[5] Ibid., 32, 33.
[6] Ibid., 43ff.
[7] Ibid., 31.
[8] CD.IV.2, 30.
[9] CD.IV (*Fragment*), 26.

creating the renewed vision within the person, so that one can live a total life of salvation toward God.

However, the change that is described is not self-generated. It is not an awakening or developing of one's own natural powers. It is wholly from God, and its intrinsic quality is different from the quality of all other changes in the individual. It is a change of one's inside, which makes one to think and act differently from the old way of life. In the language of the New Testament, it is the "new garment," the "new heart," the "new generation and birth of man."[10] It exists in sharp contrast with the old life and all what the person was. It helps one to become what he or she was not.

The history of Jesus will in no way destroy the history of the individual. What the individual receives is a new history, but it is the individual's own history. Barth raises two questions at this juncture: "How does the history of Jesus become the history of a specific person?" and "How does it become the event of one's renewing?"[11] These questions lead us to consider the divine power that is manifested both in the history of Jesus and in the life of the individual.

Divine Power in the History of Jesus

The question of 'power,' which Barth speaks about in relation to the Spirit baptism, is relevant to the discussion. The scripture speaks about the promise of power through the work of the Holy Spirit,[12] and, undoubtedly, power is a strong motif in those who search for charismatic gifts. However, Barth's understanding of power is deeply rooted in the powerful history of Jesus, which culminated in His resurrection. The history of Jesus has indwelling power because He is risen from the dead.[13] (p. 24). The resurrection is the demonstration of Christ's person and work. It was an event of great historical significance because the ultimate unleashing of the divine power was made possible in it. The Christian who lives in the here-and-now can rely on the resurrection as his or her own source of power, and, as a retrospective, can look back to this event. As prospective, it holds promise for the future in terms of eternal life, reconciliation, and one's own resurrection.

---

[10] Ibid., 8-10.
[11] Ibid., 23, 26.
[12] Acts 1:4, 5, 8
[13] CD.IV (*Fragment*), 29.

An outcome of the baptism with the Holy Spirit is the availability of the power that was first displayed in the history of Christ. It has a liberating character, because it liberates one to respond to God in the positive way, accepting the divine truth and salvation. It is this power that is at work within us, liberating us and preparing us to become responsible subjects of our own history. According to Barth, our salvation history is embedded in the history of Jesus, and our power is the power that we receive at the Baptism with the Holy Spirit.[14]

Divine Power in the Life of the Individual

It is the work of the Holy Spirit to enable the opening of a person toward God in order to receive the history of God.[15] Barth uses the conversion-initiation language to describe this special work of the Spirit. The person who was spiritually blind and deaf becomes a responsive and obedient person by the life-giving operation of the Spirit. The individual forsakes the enmity that is inherent in the physical birth and becomes a friend of God.[16]

But one must make a critical observation here. Barth fails to identify and specify the intrinsic components of the event of the Baptism of the Holy Spirit. The Spirit baptism is inextricably linked with the act of regeneration. The question that arises is: How is this experience different from the regenerating work of the Holy Spirit? What is lacking here is a clear definition of the baptism of the Holy Spirit. Even the history of Jesus is described in broader terms, which makes one not sure about how this term is rightly used in discussing a specific doctrine such as the baptism of the Holy Spirit. Although the language is too general, it nonetheless signifies and urges a deep spiritual dimension needed for our lives.

Holy Spirit Baptism Produces Freedom

The baptism with the Holy Spirit produces freedom, which enables us to be faithful to God and also to choose what God has already chosen for us. It is freedom for "that which alone is suggested as possible for him by this

---

[14] Ibid., 27.
[15] Ibid., 30.
[16] Ibid.

divine change."[17] In *Dogmatics in Outline*, Barth speaks of freedom as a necessary outcome of one's reception of the Holy Spirit.[18]

The baptism of the Spirit does not destroy human freedom, which does not become extinct in the operation of the Spirit, but rather it is maintained so that the person can act as a free moral agent before God. "Man does not fade away", says Barth, for "some other being, divine or semi-divine."[19] The Spirit baptism equips one to occupy the rightful place in relation to God. The ecstatic emotionalism that has become so much a part of modern Pentecostal movements would not be supported by Barth. Although Barth makes no direct reference to such movements, which had been gaining momentum in his days, he has this to say about the Spirit and the human freedom:

> The work of the Holy Spirit, then, does not entail the paralysing dismissal or absence of the human spirit, mind, knowledge and will. It has often been depicted thus. Attempts have been made to achieve it by strangely resigned twisting of human thought, feeling and effort. It has been overlooked that the attempt to sacrifice the human intellect and will is also an enterprise of the human spirit, that this attempt is impracticable, that the work of the Holy Spirit cannot be forced thereby, and especially that this sacrifice is not well-pleasing to God, that every intention of the Holy Spirit is to bear witness to our spirit, not to a non- human non-spirit but to the human spirit, that we are the children of God (Rom.8.16), and to help us to our feet thereby.[20]

The baptism with the Holy Spirit is central to the understanding of the Christian life. One's experience of conversion and cleansing and reorientation are all the results of the Spirit baptism. It is, in fact, the "epitome of the divine change which founds the whole Christian life."[21] For Barth, the baptism with the Holy Spirit is the beginning of the Christian life because what takes place in this event is the self-impartation of Christ.[22] This divine change, therefore, is an evidence of the presence of the grace of God, who reconciles the world to Himself. In terms of

---

[17] *Fragment*, 34.
[18] *Dogmatics in Outline*, trans. G.T. Thomson (London: SCM Press, 1949), 138.
[19] *Fragment*, 28.
[20] Ibid.
[21] Ibid., 31.
[22] This is one of the five foundational statements Barth makes about the Spirit baptism. Cf. pp. 31-33.

spirituality, the baptism of the Spirit is both meaningful and pervasive, covering almost every area of the Christian life. In Barth's view,

> baptism with the Spirit is effective, causative, even creative action on and in man. It is indeed divinely effective, divinely causative, divinely creative. Here, if anywhere, one might speak of a sacramental happening in the current sense of the term. It cleanses, renews and changes man truly and totally. Whatever may be his attitude to it, whatever he himself may make of it, it is (we recall the New Testament descriptions) his being clothed upon with a new garment which is Jesus Christ Himself, his endowment with a new heart controlled by Jesus Christ, his new generation and birth in brotherhood with Jesus Christ, his saving death in the presence of the death which Jesus Christ suffered for him.[23]

Moreover, in this special work of the Holy Spirit, there is a coming together of the full justification, sanctification, and vocation, which are ingredients of a life of salvation. The baptism takes place when Jesus enters the life of the individual as a Guarantor of God's faithfulness. In the *Fragment*, Barth returns repeatedly to the relevance of the history of Jesus for the individual Christian's experience.

Barth's Pneumatology and Christology

Barth's pneumatology and Christology are closely related. The baptism with the Holy Spirit, for Barth, is an encounter with Jesus Christ, who imparts His life to the Christian.[24] This experience leads us to the questions: What is the nature of this encounter? Is the Spirit a person who is equal in power and substance as the first two Persons of the Trinity?

On the basis of the peculiar way in which Barth brings together and identifies Christ and the Spirit, it is accurate to say that his pneumatology is determined by Christology. The Holy Spirit is the dynamic power of Jesus Christ. He is the Spirit of Christ. An important to note is the relationship between Christology and pneumatology in Barth's thought. As Rosato puts it,

---

[23] Ibid., 34.
[24] Philip J. Rosato, *The Spirit as Lord: The Pneumatology of Karl Barth* (Edinburgh: T & T Clark Ltd., 1981), 114.

Barth strives to fashion his pneumatology, or theology of personal sanctification, in line with his christology, or theology of objective justification. Only in this way can he avoid the theologically vacuous position which defines the power of grace as an innate drive inducing a person to acknowledge redemption without transforming him in the process.[25]

Barth's pneumatology is related not to anthropology or ecclesiology but to Christology. Its anthropological and ecclesiological implications can be explicated only derivatively from its Christological base.[26] Although he maintains that the Son and the Spirit are *homoousios*, sometimes he implies that the Spirit is the only the mode of presence and action of the ascended Christ. Thus, to speak of the Holy Spirit is simply to speak of the extension of the power of Christ, resulting in a close identification of Christ and the Holy Spirit. In tracing the relationship between pneumatology and Christology in Barth's thought, Thomas Smail correctly states that pneumatology is subordinate to Christology, and at times Barth achieves a total identity of the Spirit with Christ.[27] Smail, who makes an important observation about Barth's doctrine of the Spirit, has this to say:

> Christology is the objective basis of pneumatology: pneumatology is the subjective application of christology. Or, to put the same thing in terms that Barth himself likes to use, Christ is God's action in the objective realm of *being* (the Ontic realm) and the Spirit is God's action in the subjective realm of *knowledge* (the noetic realm). We participate in what God has done for us in the ontic realm in Christ, by coming to know Christ through the action of the Spirit, with the kind of knowledge that brings with it a real participation in and conformity to that which it knows.[28]

However, in the discussion of the ministry of the Holy Spirit, Barth makes a useful comment, pointing out the communication of the life of Christ to the individual at the baptism of the Spirit. Here, the Spirit is the mediator, who brings the Christian in contact with Christ. As such, the

---

[25] Ibid., 113. Also see Barth's *Dogmatics in Outline* where he declares that the Holy Spirit is the Spirit of Jesus and that the Spirit cannot be separated from Christ, because as St. Paul says, "The Lord is the Spirit" (II Cor. 3:17), 138, 139.
[26] Thomas Smail, "The Doctrine of the Holy Spirit," *Theology Beyond Christendom*, ed., John Thompson (Pennsylvania: Pickwick Publications), 1986, 91.
[18] Ibid., 93.
[28] Ibid., 96.

Spirit achieves what the Christian could not achieve, namely, a participation in the self-revelation of God. Through the faith of the believer, the Holy Spirit unites the human nature to the Word of God. He permits an individual to belong to Christ.

Barth makes every effort to distinguish between the Spirit of God and the human spirit. The Spirit of God is not identical with the human spirit. The mediating principle does not propose a merging of God and the person. There is no exaltation of the human to the divine or an overflowing of God's being into human nature. [29] Rather, an eschatological chasm exists between God and the person, and it is the function of the Spirit to cross this barrier in order to bring life to the Christian. The Spirit bridges the gap between the two and is present with human infirmities and allows one's groaning to share the efficacy of the prayer of Christ.[30] The possession of the Holy Spirit is not a natural endowment, but a gift of God. The Spirit brings light into the person's darkness and enlightens him or here so that the answer 'No' is changed to 'Yes'. The human spirit experiences freedom only when it is met by the Holy Spirit.[31] The baptism of the Spirit is thus important to the Christian life, for it grants one the ability to serve God in freedom. This freedom cannot be wrought by "human capacities or possibilities or strivings."[32]

The Spirit Baptism and Regeneration

We turn now to an important aspect of Barth's pneumatology, which received a passing mention earlier. This is the question of the relation between the Spirit baptism and regeneration. Is the baptism with the Spirit distinct from, and subsequent to, the Spirit's work of regeneration? The controversy regarding the doctrine of the Spirit baptism is centred on this question. There is no doubt concerning the efficacy of the Spirit's work of baptism by which a believer is endued with power for life and service. However, the question remains: Does the baptism of the Holy Spirit come as a "second blessing," as charismatic theologians propose? Pentecostals generally insist on a distinction between conversion and baptism of the Spirit. The second experience is similar to that of the day of Pentecost, when the apostles were filled with the Holy Spirit.

---

[29] Rosato, 28, 29.
[30] Ibid., cf. Karl Barth, *The Epistle to the Romans* (London: Oxford University Press, 1933), 314, 315.
[31] Ibid., 138, 140. St. Paul: "Where the Spirit of the Lord is, there is liberty."
[32] Ibid., 140.

According to some people, a sure sign of this subsequent work of the Spirit is the ability to speak in tongues. The problem at this point is that there are not two levels of Christians - one baptized with the Spirit and another who is not.

Barth makes no effort to distinguish between the Spirit's work of regeneration and the baptism. For him, the Spirit baptism is not a "different work, a second work alongside, behind and after the work of the reconciling covenant action of the one God accomplished in the history of Jesus Christ and manifested in his resurrection".[33] He makes several statements about the work of the Holy Spirit, and they lead us to believe that he views the baptism of the Holy Spirit and regeneration as taking place at the same time. For instance, he says:

> The foundation of the Christian life, in so far as it consists in the change effected by God, in so far as it is the self-attestation and self-impartation of Jesus Christ, and consequently baptism with the Spirit, is a form of the grace of God which actually reconciles the world to Him-the form of this grace in which it is addressed to a specific man.[34]

Contrary to the theological position held by the Pentecostal Christians, Barth speaks of this baptism as an event of conversion. It is at the baptism of the Holy Spirit that the grace of God is bestowed on the Christian. It is through this act of God that Jesus enters the life of a person in order to make that person Christian. This act changes the person radically and effectively so as to receive a new heart.[35] When Barth says that this baptism is not a "half grace or a half adequate grace" but a "whole grace and wholly adequate grace", he views this work of the Spirit as a foundational element to explain the significance of the Christian life.[36]

Barth says nothing about the gift of tongues or other gifts, a topic that normally accompanies a discussion of the Spirit baptism. For him, it is in this event, a person "acquires his Lord and Master." At this point in time, one is liberated for obedience through this experience of the "omnipotently penetrating grace.[37] This act of God liberates one from a self-enclosed state for a life in the community of other believers. Because the entire life of this person is renewed by the Spirit's work, he or she has

---

[33] *Fragment*, 29.
[34] Ibid., 33.
[35] Ibid., 34.
[36] Ibid., 35.
[37] Ibid.

to walk according to the Spirit, with whom one is baptized. This is the new life, which is totally different from the old. Therefore,

> He cannot appeal to the nexus of sin, guilt and death as the power which binds all beings, himself included, for he has been snatched from the power of this nexus by the divine change which has come upon him, in the history of Jesus Christ, in the work of the Holy Spirit.[38]

This point makes it clear that conversion and the baptism of the Holy Spirit are considered to be one act of God and that the Spirit baptism is not a second blessing.

A conclusion such as this one would be unacceptable to those who believe that the Holy Spirit baptism is distinct from and subsequent to the new birth. The Pentecostal Christians see conversion as a precondition for the Spirit baptism. Accordingly, the Spirit does not come into a believer's life in His fullness until the post-conversion experience of the Holy Spirit baptism. Therefore, one is urged to seek this experience subsequent to one's conversion, assurance of salvation, and the reception of the Spirit at regeneration.[39]

The Spirit theologies of most Charismatic and Pentecostal movements agree on this distinctive approach to the interpretation of the Scripture. Such views are inconsistent with Barth's theology. For the Pentecostals, the book of Acts is the primary source for teaching about the doctrine of the Holy Spirit. They refer especially to the events that took place on the day of Pentecost and the story of the reception of the Holy Spirit by Samaritans (Acts 8). They interpret the Samaritan incident to mean that the Samaritans who had believed and been baptized did not receive the Holy Spirit until sometime later. There was a lapse of time between the baptism of the Samaritans and their reception of the Holy Spirit. There have been several lines of interpretation of this passage either to speak for or against the baptism of the Spirit as a post-conversion experience.

One of the clearest interpretations of the Acts 8 passage is offered by James D. G. Dunn in his book *Baptism in the Holy Spirit*, in which he considers the Pentecostal interpretation to be "wholly irreconcilable" in

---

[38] Ibid., 36.
[39] Of note, however, is that there are differing opinions among the Neo-Pentecostal theologians about the time at which one receives the Spirit Baptism. It may be at conversion, or immediately after it or at other times. Cf. Christenson, Lawrence. *Speaking in Tongues and Its Significance for the Church* (Minneapolis: Bethany Fellowship, 1968), p. 38

the light of the rest of the New Testament teaching.[40] Dunn argues that if the Samaritans believed and were baptized in the name of the Lord, they must be called Christians, but if they received the Holy Spirit subsequently, they cannot be called Christians until that time. [41] According to the Bible, all whom the Spirit regenerates, He also baptizes, fills, and endows with power for ministry. This argument is biblically tenable.

However, there is a strong agreement among all Christians about the specific aim of the work of the Spirit in the Christian life. According to Barth, this experience granted by God realizes not only a divine cleansing and reorientation, but also an authorizing and equipping for ministry, which prepares Christians to become public witnesses of Jesus Christ. The ministry of witness forms the "meaning and scope of the whole of the Christian life."[42] The Spirit renews Christians by leading them into deeper conversions. This experience is only a beginning and, therefore, it does not allow one to be complacent. In Barth's thought, personal salvation, exercise of divine gifts, and the life of the Christian community are all related to one another. This perspective is clear from what he says:

> The Holy Spirit, being the Spirit of the one, but eternally rich God, is no compactly uniform mass. When He is poured forth, when men are baptized with Him, He exists in the fullness of the *Charismata* of the one community. Through their distribution each individual Christian - independently of the particularity of his natural character or personal concerns - receives his own special spiritual power and therewith his own special task in the total life and ministry of the community (cf. 1 Cor. 12 and Rom. 12).[43]

The life of a believer after the Spirit baptism is a life of fruitfulness, growth, and witness. The Christian life must always be radical just as it was in the beginning. It grows with deeper dimensions as it bears spiritual fruit in the course of the history of the Christian in the community. Barth's language in this context evokes the notion of deep

---

[40] James. D. G. Dunn, *Baptism in the Holy Spirit* (London: SCM Press, 1970). See Dunn's interpretation of the `Riddle of Samaria' based on a very convincing exegesis of the Acts passage, 55-72.
[41] Ibid., 55
[42]*Fragment*, 30, 31. Barth offers an exegesis that helps us to draw the conclusion that the experience of the Spirit baptism must lead one to a life of faithful witness to God.
[43] Ibid., 38.

spirituality, which is needed as a cure for the shallow spirituality of the contemporary Church. The work of the Spirit must be allowed to continue within the Church and in the individual person. According to Barth,

> A man is no Christian if he is not willing, ready, modest and courageous enough, so long as he lives, so long as he is given the unique opportunity, to move forward, not according to the impulses of his own heart or the fancies of his own mind, but according to the impulsion and direction of the Holy Spirit, constantly marching into a land (a small portion of the land) "that I will shew thee" (Gen. 12.1)[44]

With these words, Barth leads us into the need for growth and exercise of our newly found life in the Spirit. The present life, no matter how ripe the fruits that it bears, is not yet the perfect life that will be manifested one day. His words well up with eschatological meaning, when he says that this life is already here but not yet.[45]

Our final glory is when Christ shall return and we see Him face-to-face. This prospect instils hope into our lives for the future, while we wait for the coming of Christ. Our lives in the present must have this hope and longing, as we hasten the coming of the day of the Lord. The work of the Holy Spirit is to impel and direct Christians, to feed them with the body of Christ, to strengthen them with His blood, and to nourish and sustain them as they look forward to life eternal. Being baptized with the Holy Spirit, we undergo spiritual renewal that is also the work of the Holy Spirit in us.[46]

The Spirit's Missiologic Relevance

Barth's pneumatology in general and his doctrine of the baptism with the Holy Spirit in particular deserve our special attention in terms of its missiological importance. First of all, of note is that the pneumatological materials in the *Dogmatics* are seen in relation to the missionary work of the Christian community. In CD, IV, considerable attention is devoted to the work of the Holy Spirit and the life and witness of the Christian community.

---

[44] *Church Dogmatics* [*Fragments*], IV.4, 39.
[45] Ibid., 40.
[46] Ibid.

This emphasis is commendable, especially considering that in dogmatic thinking and writing, the outreach activity of the people of God has often been relegated to the background. Barth shows that mission belongs to the very nature and essence of the Church. There is, in his thought, a link between systematic theology and mission theology. While discussing the relation between the Spirit and the Mission, Hendrikus Berkhof points out how the main dogmatic handbooks which were produced in Europe had either entirely neglected the mission or only touched on in passing.[47] But he sees Barth as an exception to the trend. In the *Church Dogmatics* IV.3, Barth has taken a great interest in treating the whole of theology from a missionary perspective. As Berkhof adds, there is a real need for enriching systematic theology by taking in missiology. One of the problems in the theological endeavour has been, on the one hand, the institutionalization and on the other hand, an individualization of the Spirit.[48] The unfortunate neglect of this important aspect leaves theology impoverished. Berkhof's words are perceptive:

> This situation is probably to the detriment of the mission, but surely to the detriment of theology, which suffers a great impoverishment indeed in that it is oriented to situations far more than to movements. In neglecting rather than reflecting the great movement of the Spirit, it distorts the whole content of faith and is an accomplice to individualistic and institutionalistic introversion and egotism still found in the churches of today.[49]

Spirit Baptism and the Christian Witness

For Barth, Spirit baptism is important for the meaning of the Christian life, which includes the witness of the Christian community. It is the Spirit who empowers the people of God in their confession of Jesus Christ, which is their distinct action in the world. Christians are constituted by the enlightening power of the Spirit. For Karl Barth, personal salvation is not restricted to the goal of a fruitful Christian life, but a life of public witness. For he asks:

---

[47] *The Doctrine of the Holy Spirit*, (Virginia: John Knox Press, 1964), 33.
[48] Ibid., The Roman Catholic theology has the Spirit as the soul and sustainer of the church, and among the Protestants, the Spirit's work is seen in relation to personal justification and sanctification. These are opposite approaches, which render the Spirit theology static.
[49] Ibid., 34.

> Can the community of Jesus Christ ...really be only, or at any rate essentially and decisively, a kind of institute of salvation, the foremost and comprehensive medium salutis, as Calvin self-evidently assumed and said? Is not every form of egocentricity excused and even confirmed and sanctified, if egocentricity in this sacred form is the divinely willed meaning of Christian existence and the Christian song of praise consists finally only in a many-tongued but monotonous pro me, pro me, and similar possessive expressions?[50]

Concluding Critical Comments

The statement above invites a critique of Barth's thought. His pneumatology is somewhat vague as to the person of the Holy Spirit. This remains to be the perennial question in dealing with his Spirit theology. However, it does not mean that he ignores this question. He is aware that the Spirit is *homoousios*. For example, in CD.IV/1, he identifies Him to be the Spirit of God and "God Himself." He proceeds from the Father and the Son. He must be glorified together with the Father and the Son, because he is of one substance with them.[51] The Spirit unites the Father and the Son in eternal love. It is the Spirit who accomplishes the will of the Father.

In the same context, he also shows the distinct nature of the Spirit. The Spirit of God is distinct from the spirit of the world, the spirit of the community, and the spirit of the individual Christian. But one sees that Barth still speaks of the Spirit as the quickening and awakening power of Christ, which in fact creates a certain degree of vagueness about his notion of the Spirit. He says:

> It is strange but true that fundamentally and in general we cannot say more of the Holy Spirit and His work than that He is the power in which Jesus Christ attests Himself attests Himself effectively, creating in man response and obedience.[52]

Nonetheless, the *Dogmatics* is clear as to what the Spirit does in the act of reconciliation. Barth recognizes that because of pride and sinfulness, the fallen humanity is neither willing nor able to actively participate in the reconciling act of God, unless there is the work of the Holy Spirit to

---

[50] CD.IV.3, 567.
[51] Ibid., 646.
[52] CD.IV.1, 648.

awaken the human race to a new life in Christ.⁵³ The Spirit alters one's being by bringing forgiveness and peace. The Spirit guarantees the ability to recognize the change of one's situation. He incites a person to an active confession of this change through a life of lasting gratitude. It is the task of the Spirit to make the Christian community to be cognizant of its ontological relationship to Jesus Christ. As the Lord of the community, He binds them together in faith.

Barth's pneumatology is impressive, but to a certain degree it is ambiguous. He does very little to distinguish the various aspects of the Spirit theology. For example, throughout the discussion of the Baptism with the Spirit, the reader finds him presenting the work of the Spirit as inseparable from the work of Christ. This lack of distinction is a major difficulty that is observable in other parts of the *Dogmatics* as well. It is important to distinguish between the person and work of the Holy Spirit, as Abraham Kuyper has argued in his *The Work of the Holy Spirit*.⁵⁴

Another example of the confusion in Barth's pneumatology is found in his treatment of justification and sanctification. He understands justification and sanctification not as two successive acts of God, but as two moments of the one act of reconciliation. He does not favor the idea of an *ordo salutis* because he considers it an "arbitrary" and "artificial schematization,"⁵⁵ following an order of salvation that involves a descent from theology to religious and moral psychology.⁵⁶ However, he says that both justification and sanctification are not to be confused either. Justification is not sanctification, and sanctification is not justification. The one cannot replace the other.

When Barth speaks of the two momentary acts, justification is not regarded as an act accomplished once for all. They go hand-in-hand, in his scheme of thinking. This is an unusual way of representing justification because it contradicts the reality that a person is either fully justified or not justified at all. He insists on their inseparability in order to avoid the danger of self-righteousness. They go together, and one does not follow the other.⁵⁷ God's act of reconciliation is unitary and, therefore, these two acts are held together. He confuses justification and

---

⁵³ Ibid., 645.
⁵⁴ Abraham Kuyper, *The Work of the Holy Spirit* (New York: Frank & Wagnalls Company, 1900), 18-20.
⁵⁵ CD.IV.2, 501-503.
⁵⁶ Ibid.
⁵⁷ Ibid., 501.

sanctification by treating them in this peculiar way, and, as a result, the one cannot have bold assurance of one's justification. Again, for Barth, this is an attempt to rule out the possibility of either "cheap grace" on the one side, and the "self-justification," on the other.[58]

Furthermore, there is confusion in Barth's pneumatology about the doctrine of sanctification, which, for Barth, is a declarative act like justification. This view also lands one in an area of difficulty. He rightly points out that Jesus Christ is our sanctification and we become holy by participation in him. Jesus Christ is holy, and we are holy in him.[59] However, Barth fails to define and distinguish the work of the Holy Spirit apart from the work of Christ. Barth gives considerable attention to the theology of the Holy Spirit, but there is a problem that is stated well in the words of Rosato: "Christ so controls the being of the Christian that the Spirit's mediating function becomes rather lifeless."[60]

Even though Barth's pneumatology has a Christological bias and is not set forth in a language beyond ambiguity, he assigns a great deal of importance to the Spirit's work. His devoting approximately forty pages of discussion to the baptism of the Spirit in the *Fragment* is in itself a proof of this argument.

In Barth's view, the baptism of the Holy Spirit takes place in the direct self-impartation of Jesus, and it is the active and actualizing grace of God. It brings a new beginning of life, which is never complete as God's work, but moves towards a goal. The Spirit baptism reveals the power of the life to come. It awakens one for personal service. It is not a second experience after conversion, as the Pentecostal Christians believe.

Barth's language of the Spirit baptism combines the depth of scholarship and profound spirituality that inevitably are needed for the life of the Church in our own day. It reminds the Christian community of the hope of transformation and renewal, which makes them pray, *Veni Creator Spiritus*.

---

[58] Ibid.
[59] Ibid., 514 ff.
[60] Rosato, 185.

BIBLIOGRAPHY

Barth, Karl. *Church Dogmatics*, Vol. IV.1, 2, 3, 4, translated by G.W. Bromiley, Edinburgh: T & T Clark, 1956, 58, 62, 69 respectively.
------------. *Dogmatics in Outline*, trans. G.T. Thomson, London: SCM Press, 1949.
Berkhof, Hendrikus. *The Doctrine of the Holy Spirit*, Richmond, Virginia: John Knox Press, 1964.
Bruner, Frederick Dale. *A Theology of the Holy Spirit: The Pentecostal Experience and the New Testament Witness*, London: Hodder & Stoughton, 1970.
Dunn, James D.G. *Baptism in the Holy Spirit* (Studies in Biblical Theology), London: SCM Press, 1970.
Ervin, Howard M. *Conversion-Initiation and the Baptism in the Holy Spirit: An engaging Critique of James D. G. Dunn's Baptism in the Holy Spirit*, MA: Hendrickson Publishers, Inc., 1984.
Grudem, Wayne. *Systematic Theology: An Introduction to Biblical Doctrine*, Grand Rapids: Zondervan, 1994.
Hoekema, Anthony A. *Holy Spirit Baptism*, Grand Rapids, Michigan: W. B. Eerdmans Publishing Co., 1972.
Kuyper, Abraham. *The Work of the Holy Spirit*, New York: Frank & Wagnalls Company, 1900.
Moule, C.F.D. *The Holy Spirit*, London: Mowbrays, 1978.
Rosato, Philip J. *The Spirit as Lord: The Pneumatology of Karl Barth*, Edinburgh: T & T Clark Ltd., 1981.
Thompson, John. ed., *Theology Beyond Christendom (Essays on the Centenary of the Birth of Karl Barth)*, Pennsylvania, PA: Pickwick Publications, 1986.

Chapter Six

Karl Barth

A Theology of Human Work

This chapter is a theological reflection on Karl Barth's thought on human work, as explicated in *Church Dogmatics*, III.4. The purpose of this essay is to provide a basic understanding of Karl Barth's theology of human work and its relevance for today.

In Church *Dogmatics*, III.4, Karl Barth (1886-1968) sets forth a systematic and many-sided treatment of the theology of human work, a manifestation of the active life of human beings. Human life is viewed as a loan from God and therefore, it is to be lived in obedience to the call of God in Jesus Christ.

In considering human work, two considerations about God are to be presupposed at the outset. First, God is the creator, sustainer, and the provider of the cosmos. In this regard, the act of God reveals his sovereign and providential rule over all creatures. Second, God has acted redemptively in Jesus Christ by bringing salvation to humanity. Barth develops his theology of human work on this two-pronged action of God toward the created cosmos, to each of which human action must correspond. Accordingly, in order to correspond to the first case, namely, the creative and providential act of God, one must actively serve Him by proclaiming the Kingdom of God. This is the "one thing that is needful." In the second case, namely, redemption, one must work or engage in what may be called social labor. The importance of social labor lies in the maintenance of life. The divine action thus serves as the foundation for Barth's theology of work.

The Concept of Service and *Causa Dei*

Human beings are called to a life of active obedience to the command of God. God has acted and continues to act in the world, and, hence, human beings, who are created in His image, are expected to correspond to the divine action. God's action in human life calls for his people's response to Him through their actions in the world. Human life and action in correspondence to the life and action of God are not something passive or neutral, but "active, effective, and creative.[1]

People live in freedom and, therefore, they can act in a way that is different from that of all other beings. A three-fold relationship with respect to human life exists in the world: they live in relation to God, to fellow humans, and to their environment. The service they perform in this three-fold relationship is significant, because they "effect something, altering, shaping and producing" in their context.[2] Thus, human service is needed for what Barth calls the *causa Dei* or the cause of God in the world.

When this work is performed in obedience to the command of God, it has an objective, active, and affirmative character. Therefore, such actions are distinct from all that people do in the way of preserving, cherishing, and protecting life. "Inaction" and "abstention" that are commonly seen in life do not have the objective character because they are both preliminary and preparatory to the real human action, which has a "subjective direction" and an "objective achievement."[3]

The obedient life is the active life, according to Barth. No life can be said to be active unless the individuals "aim at something and achieve it." This achievement involves work, but, Barth states, "the life which is obedient to the command of God is much more than work" (p. 473): the concept of service required of Christians has to be seen from the vantage point of the Kingdom of God. God's redemptive action in the person and work of Jesus Christ is presupposed in human service. The service performed for the furtherance of God's Kingdom itself is work, and it pertains to the *Kerygma*, which occupies the centre of all human actions. It is for this service that God called, justified, sanctified, and conferred on us the blessings of the Kingdom. The meaning and purpose of all human actions in the world can be viewed in terms of this correspondence. No one can appropriately and diligently correspond to the action of God, unless God so prepares him for this response.

The doctrine of sanctification is important in this respect. Barth sees it as a restorative activity, aimed at re-establishing the human capacity to serve God.[4] As an essential activity in the provision of divine salvation, sanctification becomes a foundational principle that inspires human

---

[1] *Church Dogmatics* III.4, 470.
[2] Ibid.
[3] Ibid., 471.
[4] Ibid., 474.

service and whereby God quickens the "new man," created in Christ Jesus for good works.

Characteristics of Human Service

The objective character of human service has a "sufficient range of meaning to describe from all angles the human action which correspond to the divine" (475). A person's service implies choice, freedom to execute a deliberation, and, above all, the ability to act in response to the choice and action of God. Here human choice before a sovereign God means not only the choosing of Yahweh but also the rejecting of another lord. And it is this definitive human choice that makes one righteous, according to Barth. However, this human choice can be made only as it has been prompted first by the divine choice.

In Barth's thought, freedom plays an important role in our worship and service, and it is essential to the free expression of self in human action. The rationale for this is found in scripture:

> To serve Yahweh is evidently the direct meaning of the free existence which Israel does not have in Egypt and cannot secure for itself, but which is finally attained for it by the judgment of Yahweh on Pharaoh and his people. To serve Him is to be this people delivered by God and to do what corresponds to this deliverance and has to be done as a matter of course on the basis of Israel's freedom.[5]

In order for one to understand the significance of service, one has to see Christ as the suffering Servant who came to the earth "not to be served but to serve and to give his life as a ransom for many."[6] The God who is worthy to receive all worship and service of both men and angels appearing as Servant himself is an example of service. This dimension of service constituted in the incarnate ministry of Christ is the supreme model of service, because what is comprehended in Christ is the kenotic love of God for the sake of man's redemption. There is no better paradigm of service that is appropriate and exemplary. To explain it in the words of Moltmann:

> Through pain, work, and self-renunciation God accomplishes the deliverance of imprisoned humanity. Work and servanthood

---

[5] Ibid., 476.
[6] Mk. 10:45

> become the embodiment of God's liberating and delivering action. Through servanthood God comes to his lordship in the world.[7]

According to Barth, to serve God means to serve him as Christ served, and to follow God means "to follow His way of service, of the total service which in relation to the world in which it is rendered may include the surrender of life itself and must certainly include the readiness for it."[8] The service that is required of one is to be performed in participation in God's commission for men and women. This is how one may know whether or not it is really God's service, because there are those who go their own ways and live for themselves under the pretext of a self-chosen service.[9] In other words, genuine service should be offered in the context of, or in relation to, the people of God. This understanding of service comes at the root of Christian community in Barth's theology of work. Human beings are a counterpart in God's cosmic activity. They are to be "mobilized and thrown into action in participation in the doing of this will and work." But this human participation does not make him what Barth calls a "co-creator, co-saviour, or a co-regent in God's activity."[10]

Nonetheless, Barth notes the distinction that exists between what is of God and what is of humans. The human agency can never accomplish the divine will on its own. The Christian cannot serve in his or her strength but only in the strength that God provides. However, whatever one accomplishes receives the commendation of God when the activity is underlined and attested by faith.

The cause of God is the primary goal of service. Service is the essential character of human activity by which one can fulfil obligations of being in covenant with God. The Christian community is the most appropriate context, in Barth's view, to help one perform service to the cause of God: He asks:

> If service is the true and essential character of human activity, and if this character is displayed where it is rendered to the cause of God, why should it not be practical supremely and properly as the activity of the Christian community? Is not this activity supremely practical, and therefore in no sense alien in

---

[7] Jürgen Moltmann, "The Right to Meaningful Work," *On Human Dignity*, M. Douglas Meeks, ed. (Philadelphia: Fortress Press, 1984), 44.
[8] *Church Dogmatics*, III.4, 477.
[9] Ibid.
[10] Ibid., 482.

the highest and truest sense?[11]

Hence, the active service required of the Christian becomes the active service of the community. Every member of the community has to emerge from neutrality into the service performed for the cause of God, which is found in Jesus Christ. Each one must use the gifts and talents to witness to the grace of God and thus fulfil the task of kerygma.

Community, in Barth's view, is constituted by individuals who are united together by a common meaning, task, and purpose, which inevitably are linked with the meaning, task, and purpose of the Kingdom of God. The Christian community has no reason for existence other than what God has intended.[12] It is composed of people who confess and hold to the same meaning, which is effective in leading them in the service of the Kingdom. This redemptive task should occupy the center of all human actions.

Work as *Parergon*

Barth denies that the modern Western civilization has derived its work ethic from the Bible. Work is important, but it does not receive the central place in his theology. In his words:

> It is obvious that Jesus of the Synoptics and the Fourth Gospel cannot be claimed in support of this high estimation of work. He certainly assumed, as His parables indicate, that secular labour of all sorts and kinds belongs to the life of man and must be undertaken by him. On the other hand, there can be no evading the awkward fact that He never called anyone directly to this type of work. On the contrary He seems to have summoned His disciples away from their secular work.[13]

What were more important to both Jesus and the Apostle Paul than anything else were their Kingdom activities. Although he was a carpenter, there is no evidence in the Scripture that Jesus continued this work after he had commenced the messianic ministry. What Paul did in order to maintain life during his ministry was "done on the margin of his

---

[11] CD.III.4, 485.
[12] Ibid., 513.
[13] Ibid., 472.

apostolic existence,"[14] and he had no positive interest either in work or its achievements.

Even in the creation account Barth sees no calling for cultivation. In the Old Testament, "work was a self-evident necessity of life."[15] Thus, the Protestant work ethic is biblically untenable. On the contrary, "the necessity of work, at least in the form which we know it and do it is reckoned among the consequences of the curse of sin in Genesis 3:17," the reality of which is expressed by the preacher in Ecclesiastes who portrays nothing but the hopelessness and weariness of work. Moreover, the Decalogue contains no positive command to work, whereas it commands man to rest on the Sabbath.

This explanation should not prompt anyone to think that Barth disparages human work. In his scheme of thinking, work has its place among other things humans are commanded to do. The older Protestant work ethic came as a reaction to the medieval overestimation of the *vita contemplativa* of meditation, prayer, and worship in a state of absolute obedience in contrast to the *vita activa*. The latter is consistent with the teachings of the Bible, but the problem arises when it is applied only to secular work. It was the Kingdom activity that was more important to Jesus. Therefore, "[t]his simple thing is the human act in the supreme and most concrete sense."[16] And it is to this that Christ called his disciples from all other works.

The theology of work that is distinguished from the service of the Kingdom is based on the foundation of the doctrine of providence. The divine work of providence includes not only the preservation of creation but also the divine government by which God exercises his rule over every "world-occurrence." In the words of the Apostle Paul, "we live and move and have our being" (Act. 17:28).

God's work of providence is not futile or inactive, but is "caring, effective and energetic and always active."[17] Barth suggests this point of correspondence when he says that "God does His work as Creator with the intention that man should respond by doing his work as creature." This correspondence reveals itself when man places himself at God's disposal, and it is for this he is "sanctified, summoned and determined." He is under obligation and therefore he cannot be "refractory, indifferent,

---

[14] Ibid.
[15] Ibid.
[16] Ibid., 487.
[17] John Calvin, *The Institutes of Christian Religion,* Tony Lane and Hilary Osborne, ed (London: Hodder & Stoughton, 1986).

neutral nor passive". He is called to exercise and fulfil this obligation in the creaturely freedom which has been granted to him."[18]

Barth's discussion reveals a teleological motif in the divine providence: "God intervenes for the world," and "He cares for its continuance for the existence and welfare of the creatures." God governs and directs all things in creation to an appointed end. In other words, God rules all things teleologically so as to secure the accomplishment of His purpose. God is the King of the cosmos, and we should work in accordance with His purpose and rule. The human lordship over the creation is derived from the Lordship of Christ. It has a goal inasmuch as it corresponds to the divine act of providence. Thus:

> As therefore, the work of divine providence does not take place for its own sake but in that teleological connexion [sic], so man's work cannot be done for its own sake but only in the teleological connexion [sic] which it is given by God.[19]

The divine government, as an activity of providence, embraces all of God's creatures from the beginning. While it is universal, it descends to particulars, whether they seem to be insignificant or accidental, or whether they be good or evil deeds of men. As God's love, care, and interest are seen in every part of the creation, nothing can be withdrawn from His government. All of creation enjoys the benefits of God's rule as He sustains, preserves, and maintains it.

A relation exists between creation and covenant in the context of the providence: "if covenant is the internal basis of the creation, creation is the external basis of the covenant." Thus, Christians in their covenant relationship fulfil their responsibility in creation. Therefore:

> As God sees to His creature, and cares for it, in order that it may not cease as the object of His love, He requires of man the action corresponding to this care and providence. Addressing and claiming him as His Covenant-partner, or, we may now say correctly, as a member of the Christian community, He also commands him- in order to make this possible to exist as His human creature, requiring that his active life should take this human form, and fulfil itself in this form. Work is this human form.[20]

---

[18] CD.III.4, 475.
[19] Ibid., 521.
[20] Ibid., 517.

Human work is meaningful for affirming one's existence as God's creature. Work helps in the preservation and maintenance of life on earth, so that people can live and respond to the redemptive action of God and thus become recipients of the grace of God.

> The preservation, guaranteeing, and continuation of life demand that man should work, that he should integrate himself at some point into the great system of ends in which the interpenetration of spirit and nature is always sought under the most varied historical conditions.[21]

Human work is a "synthesis" of man as a unity of "soul and body, nature and spirit, and of inner and outer reality, of reason and organized substantiality."[22] The individual exists as a unity. In this ordered unity of soul and body, a person has to work for the sake of the service required of him or her.

Barth also describes human work as "incidental," stating that it is required of the person because it is a "necessary prerequisite of his service." Barth calls this *parergon*. All human work is the fulfilment of this ordered unity in which, as a creature, one affirms oneself as the "soul of his body and the body of his soul". This expression of human person in work is termed synthesis.[23]

The one who thus works in accordance with the requirement of divine providence will "emerge from a vegetatively somatic life, from a distinct and abstract externality." Work helps one come out of a "purely psychic existence." In work, one affirms, wills and realizes oneself in one's totality. In work one has opportunity not only to express oneself but also to know oneself, of one's centrality and meaning in creation. There is a law of human nature that is fulfilled in work which is done in obedience to the command of God. Nevertheless, what is done by human hands remains human. It is neither an extension of the divine activity nor an act of creation but a "movement within the created order."[24]

---

[21] Barth, *Ethics*, 218.
[22] CD.III.4, 518.
[23] Ibid., 519.
[24] Ibid., 520.

Human Work and Culture

Human culture is produced in work, but what is produced by the synthesis of soul and body is never done for its own sake. It is not autonomous and, therefore, it cannot declare itself independent from the overall goal that God has established.

The human culture is present only in the event of man's work. Thus, its nature is earthly and creaturely and does not have a divine character. It can conceal or replace heaven only by way of illusion. Because of the earthly and creaturely character of work, participation in it is not participation in the divine work. Thus in Barth's view, human work cannot be done for its own sake, as he makes it clear that

> No independent meaning of work, no intrinsic necessity, can be proved in the framework of Christian ethics. On the contrary, the idea of an independent value and existence of human culture, and consequent requirement of work for work's sake, can only be dismissed.[25]

The importance of faith for acceptable human work can never be underestimated. Faith and its obedience must serve as the foundation of all human action and without faith, work "stands under the shadow of the most profound uncertainty."[26]

This position raises an important question: what is the value of work accomplished by non-Christians? In Barth's thought, there is a decisive difference between the work accomplished by Christians and that accomplished by non-Christians. However, he does not depreciate the work that is done even without knowing its meaning and necessity. Such works are established by divine providence. They fall in the "nexus of God's will." They are justified as they occur in the world, which is created and ruled by the sovereign will of God. Every person is equipped by God for active self-affirmation and, thus, whether realizing it or not is involved in what is needed as preparation for the coming of the Kingdom of God. Hence, God makes use of the labour of even non-Christians, which also helps them to achieve a degree of independence in livelihood and to be a giver instead of an unlawful recipient.

Further, work is not just any activity or labour for the procuring of the various means of livelihood. It is unethical to earn one's livelihood

---

[25] Ibid., 523.
[26] Ibid.

through "falsehood and deception" or through illegitimate means. Barth shows that some works are not harmful or abominable in themselves, although they may be very different from what is demanded by God, and that all work is subject to being judged by biblical and ethical criteria. Work that is demanded by God is the "human form of prolonging."[27] But human action that prolongs life but disregards humanity is not true and honest work.

Criteria for Judging Human Work

Barth offers some ethical criteria to judge human work. According to the criterion of objectivity, one can set goals and achieves them, consistent with the rules that are present in every purpose. One works rightly only by committing oneself to these rules, "immersing" in and "orientating" to them.

For Barth, true work is consistent with justice, whereas "botched work" is not right, or righteous, work. One must ask questions about the nature and integrity of work to determine if his or her work does justice to each specific task and means.

True work also must be measured on the basis of human worth. One has to determine how much of the work contributes to the advancement, improvement, and amelioration of human existence. Human worth and honesty are determined by "what is willed and purposed and effected, i.e., by whether human existence is served, or not served, or perhaps even ignored by it."[28] Thus, in Barth's view, honest and true work is that which makes a significant and just contribution to human existence. Some works are neither "useful nor harmful" because they are directed to "neither good nor evil," and whereas determining the worthiness of some work is not easy, Barth suggests:

> To the question whether a certain type of work is worthy or unworthy, a different answer might have to be given at different times and places, from different standpoints and for different people.[29]

The third criterion of human work is the humanity involved in work. When we work to earn our daily bread, we must do so in the fellowship

---

[27] Ibid., 527.
[28] Ibid., 530.
[29] Ibid., 533.

of others who are in the same situation. "Co-operation" and a respectful "co-existence" are required. Barth would deny the unhealthy competition that is so prevalent in the modern industrial world. The humanity of human work is lost when there is greed and "isolation and abstraction of one's own needs, wishes and desires while deliberately thwarting and ignoring those of others." To stand in opposition to one's own fellow-beings at work is a mark of injustice and inhumanity, indicating the thoughtlessness involved when we think we can work apart from being in fellowship with others who have the same needs and aims. Because the exploitative tendencies and competitions that are so widespread in work situations create hostility and isolation, we are to be restrained by the command of God, and only then will work occur in obedience to God and in peace with one another.[30]

The last criterion is that of limitation. According to this criterion, true work is that which done after one had rested from all his work. It is then one does one's work aright.

Barth also sees an internal work as being an important preliminary to the external work. This internal work is the "planning, pondering and designing" that are needed for the efficient performance of the external work. A person is both soul and body and, therefore, work must be done both within and without. The criterion of reflectivity in this case is no less important than the external work itself. In his view:

> If reflection is to be carried through, it demands an effort which can be much greater than that of a woodcutter, factory director, or university professor. For reflection demands honesty, courage and consistency at a point where we would rather be dishonest, cowardly and inconsistent, namely, in solitude. It demands rest where we would rather rush into cheerful or tragic unrest because in rest we might have to face the truth.[31]

Vocation

Barth shows that vocation is related to the coming of God's Kingdom because it corresponds to the divine calling. It is the "limited place of responsibility at which he must always be found." One's vocation does not exhaust in one's profession, because it is "no more than true than

---

[30] Ibid., 546.
[31] Ibid., 550.

God's calling which comes to him is simply an impulsion to work."³² It does not come into line with social labor as such, to the mere maintenance of human life, but rather to the need for transformation of the social world, of which social labor is one part.³³

Accordingly, the most significant aspect of human work is not the wholehearted participation in the pattern of social labour, but Christian action to change its dehumanizing character.³⁴ The Christian's work has the power to reform labour situations. To use the words of Moltmann:

> In its works worldwide Christianity follows its divine call and fills the whole world with the charismata of the new creation; reformation is the beginning of the eschatological *reformatio mundi*.³⁵

In Barth's understanding, there is an "external limitation" to one's vocation that has a "corresponding internal limit.³⁶ The external limitation is one's historical situation and no Christian be indifferent to the divine calling in his or her historical situation, because "this historical situation is also part of the vocation of man."³⁷

The internal limit is the personal endowment, aptitude, and inclination. One has to accept the situation and not run from it. No situation is better or worse, more exalted or lower, than others. This limitation is not blind fatalism whereby man is glued to the wheel of his oppressive situation, as the case may be, in a hopeless and pessimistic way. The historical situation is not to be understood as "determination." Rather, it is in one's situation that one answers the call of God and proves to be faithful to God. To use the language of Moltmann, vocations are historical, changeable, limited by time, and directed toward neighbour and society. They are "undertaken, shaped, and changed according to the call." Vocations are not "crippling prisons" but "possibilities and opportunities for hope and action."³⁸

A notable aspect of Barth's theology of work is the importance he gives to rest, which he considers a prior necessity of work. In order for the

---

³² Ibid., 599
³³ Paul West, "Karl Barth's Theology of Work: A Resource for the Late 1980s," *Modern Churchman*, 30 (1988):17.
³⁴ Ibid.
³⁵ Jürgen Moltmann, *On Human Dignity* (Philadelphia: Fortress Press, 1984), 45.
³⁶ CD.III.4, 618, 623.
³⁷ Ibid., 618.
³⁸ Moltmann, 48.

Christian to undertake his work in accordance with the command of God, he must pause, rest, and keep the holy day in the sight of God. Rest is a "solemn interruption," and this paradoxical "activity" of the holy day is the origin of all other activity. As Barth points out, God rested on the Sabbath and this day is our first day. Human history under the command of God really begins with rest and not with work, with celebration of God-given freedom and not with a required task, with Sunday and not with a working day.[39]

We are created in the first place to participate in God's freedom and rest and not to work. Because God blessed the seventh day, man should without any merit or work rest with God before he goes to work. Then he will find the grace promised him from the beginning of his existence.

Concluding Critical Comments

Karl Barth's idea of human work has implications for our times. His criticism of the thoughtlessness of human work is relevant. The thoughtless attitude in work and industry, as is seen in our world, does not do justice to God, to others, or to the one who performs the work. If right work is righteous work, this ethical dimension is absent in the modern technological society. For example, Western society has patterned and adjusted itself into a consistent and goal-oriented system in the promotion of economic and technological progress. As a result, it exerts permanent stress and creates tension and restlessness on human lives. The individual has become an object of progress. In this process, the human personality is changed due to inner tension and uncertainty. The Western man has developed a wholehearted trust in progress, which has become a substitute for religion. Economic progress is entirely defined apart from qualitative criteria and is reduced to what is directly and quantitatively measurable.

Instead of technology being adjusted to the humanity of workers, we are apparently encountering a situation in which workers, in body and soul, are being adjusted to technology. In Barth's language, it is an inhuman situation that eventually produces internal disintegration. Justice is essential to the understanding of human work, according to Barth. In our modern industrial culture, the division of labour and the intense process of mechanization deprive the workers of human choice, creativity, co-operation, and mutual contact with fellow-beings.

---

[39] Ibid., 52.

Human work cannot be done for its own sake, nor can it be done without faith and obedience. Work must be done in correspondence to the goal and commands of God. Human beings cannot declare themselves autonomous nor can their work be reduced to one aspect but always must be seen in the larger context of God's Kingdom.

This concept is particularly important in the areas of natural and human sciences, where created reality is reduced to one aspect without referring to the overall meaning and teleological connection. This reductionism breaks the coherence and indissoluble unity of God's creation. It tries to conceal or replace heaven by illusion. The work of human beings is to express their gifts and talents as a celebration of God's glory.

BIBLIOGRAPHY

Barth, Karl. *Church Dogmatics*, III. 4. Bromiley, G.W. and Torrance, T.F., eds., Edinburgh: T. & T. Clark, 1961.

-----------. *Ethics*. Braum, D., ed, G.W. Bromiley, trans. New York: The Seabury Press, 1981.

Moltmann, Jürgen. *On Human Dignity*. Philadelphia: Fortress Press, 1984.

West, Paul. "Karl Barth's Theology of Work: A Resource for the Late 1980s," *Modern Churchman*, 30, 1988.

Chapter Seven

Bernard J. F. Lonergan, S. J.

The Notion of Communications in the Theological Method

Bernard J. F. Lonergan, S.J., (1904-1984) was an important figure in the 20th century Roman Catholic theology. His writings, ranging from philosophical issues to theological method, have inspired many religious scholars and ministers throughout the world. He also engaged issues in mathematics, science, and economics, usually thought to be outside the immediate confines of theology. Lonergan's works reveal a particular concern for method in theology and the other disciplines mentioned above. His method proposes a framework for doing theology in a creative way, instead of providing certain rules to be followed blindly.

The main purpose of this essay is to examine Lonergan's notion of 'Communications,' which is an integral part of his theological method. The primary source for this study is his well-known work *Method in Theology*.[1] What I propose to do here is to extract from this work those strands that deal with the idea of communications and to discuss them in a manner that is relevant to the ministry of the church. I am fully aware that extracting any one strand from a method tends to untie the entire material of the work, on account of its intricate argument.[2] However, such attempts to focus on the select specialties had been made successfully by other scholars.[3]

---

[1] *Method in Theology* (United Kingdom: Dayton Longman & Todd, Ltd, 1971). The present discussion, which uses an informal writing style, is based on the reprint of the second edition provided by University of Toronto Press, Toronto, 1990.
[2] Elizabeth Maclaren, "Theological Disagreement and Functional Specialties," *Looking at Lonergan's Method*, Patrick Corcoran, ed. (Dublin: Talbot Press, 1975), 73.
[3] See Wolfhart Pannenberg, "History and Meaning in Bernard Lonergan's Approach to Theological Method," in Patrick Corcoran's work cited above.

Lonergan's method is called *transcendental*. He begins his work with a description of method in general and the transcendental method is particular. His method is a "normative pattern of recurrent and related operations" that produces "cumulative and progressive results." [4] Whereas other methods aim to meet exigences and exploit opportunities specific to particular fields, the transcendental method "is concerned with meeting the exigences and exploiting opportunities presented by the human mind itself."[5] However, transcendental method is only part of theological method, as he concedes. It provides the basic anthropological component, but not the specifically religious component. This is why he suggests that we add a consideration of religion,[6] and that is what he is doing in Chapter Four of *Method*.

Lonergan's theological method carries eight steps or functional specialties, of which communications is the final step. These steps are related to each other and are to be seen as stages in the process. Two things must be said about the functional specialties. *First*, they are arrived at by "distinguishing and separating stages of the process from data to results,"[7] rather than by dividing the field of data. *Second*, the functional specialties are related to four levels of consciousness, namely, empirical, intellectual, rational, and moral. In the chapter on religion, Lonergan also introduces the notions of a downward movement and an upward movement in consciousness. In the first movement, love precedes knowledge to complement the upward movement. In the second, knowledge precedes love. To sum up this section, these four levels of consciousness and the two movements constitute the eight functional specialties in Lonergan's method, in which research and communications are empirical in nature, interpretation and systematic are intellectual, history and doctrines are rational, and dialectics and foundations are moral. Another way of looking at them is: research, interpretation, history, and dialectics comprise the positive and creative phase of theology; foundations, doctrines, systematic, and communications form the normative and healing phase. They hinge on what is called *conversion* (See Chapter Five for a detailed discussion).

The first seven steps are research, interpretation, history, dialectic, foundations, doctrines, and systematics. A brief comment on each of the first seven stages is in order. In research, data are collected for theological

---

[4] *Method*, 14.
[5] Ibid.
[6] Ibid., 25.
[7] Ibid., 126.

investigation. In the second stage, the gathered data are interpreted in their historical context, understanding especially what the author had in mind when the material was written. History can be either general or specific. As an integral part of theology, its major concern is to understand the doctrinal history of Christian theology. In dialectic, we deal with the concrete, the dynamic, and the contradictory. Therefore, it finds a great deal of information in the Christian movements. Theology receives its foundations through an objectification of conversion, and as Lonergan puts it, conversion is "existential, intensely personal, utterly intimate."[8] Doctrines deal with judgments of fact and of value. The seventh specialty, systematics, works at appropriate systems of conceptualization, to remove apparent inconsistencies and move towards some grasp of spiritual matters.[9]

It is in the final stage of communications that Christian theology bears fruit. This stage brings the Church into the area of practical theology, which deals with the dissemination of the Christian message and with the formulation of policies relating to ecclesiology and missiology. Lonergan's method raises ecumenical and interreligious issues that are relevant to the field of communications, whether it be in one's own culture or in an alien culture. The final stage of communications brings theologians, ministers, and Christian educators together to work out the ultimate transpositions of the Gospel in the daily life and ministry of the Church.

At the center of the Christian message is the Gospel and it is this Gospel that is to be communicated both in the immediate and remote contexts of the Church. Communications in various forms and levels deal with the transposition of the message from the world of theory to the world of cultural realities, where people can understand and experience it.

The Christian Message as 'Meaning'

According to Lonergan, the Christian message is 'meaning' and meaning is cognitive, constitutive, and effective. To communicate is to impart meaning between individuals or between cultures. It may take place in many forms, such as intersubjectively, symbolically, artistically, linguistically, and incarnately[10] Meaning cannot be transmitted effectively

---
[8] Ibid., 130.
[9] Ibid., 132.
[10] Ibid., 78.

apart from communications in any or all of these forms. It is through successful communications that individual meaning becomes common meaning for the community. Common meaning takes shape over many generations, as each generation, with its own contribution to it, passes it on to the successive generations. The message that the Church communicates to the world is, then, passed from one generation to another generation, and, through various forms of communication, invites others to share in the meaning of the Gospel. Three things are to be noted here.

First, to be cognitive is to have the data or facts so that one may believe and enlarge one's horizon. Research, the first step in the methodology, is to gather data. Insofar as the message is cognitive, it is real. Appropriation of truth, as Lonergan says elsewhere, has relation to one's cognitional activity.[11] Through such activity one makes truth one's own, as the areas of one's understanding of doctrines and systematics are illuminated. Cognition takes one from the realm of the infant into the realm of the adult, from an immediate world of sensory perceptions into a world mediated by meaning. The infant's world lacks any "perceptible intrusion from insight or concept, reflection or judgment, deliberation or choice." [12] A cognitive message transmits concepts, insights, and judgments that enable one to know, judge, and deliberate. The Church's message to the world is replete with facts that are vital for the hearer's understanding of the Gospel and God's love.

Second, the Christian message should be constitutive. It constitutes the community and facilitates the experience of *koinonia*. It is a vital function of meaning as it pertains to the reality of the person or community or group. It is a given that every social or political institution in any given culture is constituted by meaning. For example, there is meaning in religion, art, language, science, and philosophy. Each institution in human culture can change with the change of its meaning, as it is not an immutable and fixed entity. These institutions develop and progress in accordance with new and changing circumstances. For example, political, social, and cultural transformations take place when there is a change of concept, idea, or evaluation or reinterpretation or judgment. This is true of church, family, state, constitution, law, and all other entities. Sociopolitical changes such as revolutions, overthrow of governments, displacement of people, and so forth can be explained in terms of the

---

[11] *Insight: A Study of Human Understanding* (London: Longman's, Green & Co. Ltd., 1957), 55.
[12] Ibid., 76.

change of meaning that a given culture may experience. Thus, the transformation of a Christian community results from the constitutive nature of the message to which they are committed.

In Lonergan's thought, the Christian message is "constitutive in as much as it crystallizes the hidden inner gift of love into overt Christian fellowship."[13] The Christian life is a manifestation of the gift of God. The constitutive element of the message is the "I believe…" part that declares a person's commitment to the cognition. None of these elements should remain a theoretical abstraction, although such abstraction may prove to be a good intellectual exercise for some. In the final analysis, these abstractions may be useless unless one practices the belief. This simply means that those who preach the message must first of all *know* the message and *practice* the message themselves.

According to Lonergan, communication is not repeating some conserved data (for such people do not know the message) but it is a dynamic, experiential, and purposeful activity. In other words, we should be both authentic and responsible in our communication of the Christian message. This is clear when he says:

> For without living the Christian message one does not possess its constitutive meaning; and one cannot lead another to share what one oneself does not possess. Finally, those that communicate the effective meaning of the Christian message, must practice it.[14]

Third, the Christian communications must be effective. Considerable investigating, planning, consulting, and policy-making are needed in the Church to make the process of communication effective. They are meaningful events in the overall structure,[15] and they help train men and women whose task it is to invite people to the unconditional love of God. Lonergan tells us that "the Christian message is effective inasmuch as it directs Christian service to human society to bring about the kingdom of God." [16] Thus, we can say that the purpose of the Church's communication is the furtherance of God's kingdom.

---

[13] *Method*, 362.
[14] Ibid.
[15] Ibid., 78.
[16] Ibid., 362.

Communications and Community

Communications give rise to community and the community perfects itself through subsequent communication. The Christian community is an incarnation of Christian meaning, and it is a society of all those who have experienced conversion and have been transformed by the message of Christ. It shares a common faith and religious experience. The Word and the gift of God's love result in their koinonia, witness, and service.[17]

Lonergan states that "common meaning is potential, formal, actual, realized by decisions and choices.[18] These choices affect the degrees of achievement in a community depending on how members remain authentic to the held values. The contradictory understanding, judgment, and experience may contribute to the disintegration of the community. Accordingly, "Community coheres or divides, begins or ends, just where the common field of experience, common understanding, common judgments, common commitments begin and end."[19] Whenever the common meaning is lost, people stay out of touch. When a common way of understanding is absent in a community, people live in different "worlds"begin to misunderstand, to distrust, to suspect, to fear, and even resort to violence; when common judgments are lacking, people live in different worlds.

Common meaning, for Lonergan, is doubly constitutive because it is constitutive of the individual as a *member* of the community, as well as constitutive of the community itself.[20] Therefore, there must be continuous and consistent process of communications of the people who share the same cognitive, constitutive, and effective meaning. The common meaning constitutes the community, and divergent meaning divides it. Such divisions are expressed through cultural diversity and class differences. The most serious division is produced by the presence or absence of intellectual, moral, and religious conversion. Hence, communication in the forms of preaching and teaching is vital to the experience of conversion. Scripturally, it is the preaching of the Word that brings salvation.[21]

---

[17] Ibid., 363.
[18] Ibid., 79.
[19] Ibid.
[20] Ibid., 357.
[21] Rom. 10:14, 15.

Redemptive Communication

The message that the Church communicates is redemptive in nature. Lonergan describes the Church as a redemptive, structured, and outgoing process that embodies structured meaning. God's gift of His love and the message of Christ are fundamental to the Church. Thus, its members enrich one another through fellowship and service. In order to facilitate the communication of the Christian message, the Church must train its members to utilize their gifts and talents. It promotes the good order in which needs of people are met "regularly, sufficiently, and efficiently."[22]

The Christian Church has a special interest in the spiritual transformation of its members by the experience of Christ's love both in relation to God and in relation to other members of the society. Interpersonal communications within the Church community are important not only for the active life and service of the Church but also for the maturing of spiritual gifts within the community.

The Church is also an outgoing process, and it reaches out to the whole world. It does not exist for itself but for the world that is in need of God's love and service. The aim of its outreach is the realization of God's Kingdom in the world, just as much as it experiences the kingdom within its own fold. The Gospel is universal in character and, therefore, the outreach has to be planned from a global perspective. A church that does not go beyond itself or does not transcend itself is not a genuine church. The Church should proclaim the message of Christ (i.e., his incarnation, his cross, his suffering, death, burial, and resurrection). It invites others to receive His grace and forgiveness.

The redemptive message that the Church preaches must have two essential components, according to Lonergan. The Christian message "tells not only of God's love but also of man's sin."[23] One exposes and addresses the sinfulness and inauthentic living of human beings, and the other expounds the self-emptying love of Christ. In other words, one has an anthropocentric focus delineating the tragedy of man resulting from his inauthentic living, and the other has a Christocentric focus offering the solution to his tragedy. One is problem-posing, and the other is problem-solving. Because of sin, alienation, and ideology that destroy the human community, these two elements are inevitable in any effective

---

[22] *Method*, 363.
[23] Ibid., 364.

proclamation of the Christian message. Conversion is the way to self-transcendence.[24]

The refusal of self-transcendence results in alienation from man's true self. The basic form of ideology is the self-justification of the alienated man, and ideology corrupts minds [25] and destroys the social good. Conversion results in progress, whereas ideology that results from sin generates moral and personal decline. This is where the redemptive message of the Church becomes very relevant. Through its communications, the Church helps in conversion, which produces in the human a change of intent, change of mind, and change of direction.[26] Human errors, rationalization, ideologies, and inauthentic living will fall by the experience of conversion. According to Lonergan, there is a need for discerning and addressing the ideologies that corrupt human minds and society.

Indeed, ideology can be an entire system of values, convictions, and norms that are used for reaching seemingly legitimate ends. It can become a kind of religion with its own new source of meaning and selfish end. It creates new gods that force their will on human societies and finally destroy them. It is the Gospel of Christ that has power to undo the evil brought about by sin. Lonergan suggests that the Church must coordinate plans in all areas of its life and deploy its resources. The mission of the Church is to communicate redemptively, which means proclaiming the Gospel in diverse forms with the deep dimension needed for the challenges posed by human sin. This proclamation is a call to repent and to be reconciled to one's Creator, to himself, and to the world.

Gospel and Human Culture in Communication

In Lonergan's understanding, a difference exists between communicating the Gospel and communicating the Gospel as it has been developed in one's own culture. [27] This useful distinction between the two proclamations helps us keep intact the integrity of the Gospel without too closely identifying it with the culture. A distinction of this kind, as proposed by Lonergan, is not always easy to make because one has always experienced the Gospel in one's own cultural milieu. However, when one fails to distinguish between the two, the Gospel would appear

---

[24] Ibid., 357.
[25] Ibid., 55.
[26] Ibid., 52.
[27] Ibid., 362.

to be an "alien patch" on another culture. According to Lonergan's suggestion, the Gospel must be communicated in such a way that it becomes a "line of development within the culture."[28] Preaching the Gospel as it has been developed in one's own culture runs the risk of asking others to renounce their culture and accept the alien culture, a mistake that has occurred frequently in the history of cross-cultural missions. Lonergan rightly discourages this tendency of "superimposing" one's culture on others, as it would "disrupt" that culture.

Although one preaches the Gospel the way one understands it, lives it, and experiences it in one's own cultural milieu, when the presentation of the Gospel has been too closely associated with a particular missionary's culture, many crosscultural difficulties have developed. One must understand that if the Gospel is too influenced by the customs and ways of a person's life, it results in the loss of the Gospel's identity. Through careful exercise of discernment, the Church is to preach the Gospel, not the Gospel and the culture.

The Christian message is transcultural in scope and, therefore, the communication of the Gospel must be global[29] in order to create a global Christian community. Both human knowing and feeling are incomplete without expression. The effects of sin and alienation are universal. Therefore, the Gospel must be preached not only in one's own culture but to all cultures and nations. There is a longing for transcendence in every culture, and in every culture people experience the gift of God's love. Jesus emphasized the process of communication when he commanded his disciples to "Go into all the world and preach the Gospel." Appropriate manners and methods are to be sought in communicating transculturally. In Lonergan's words,

> God's gift of his love (Rom. 5.5) has a transcultural aspect. For if this gift is offered to all men, if it is manifested more or less authentically in the many and diverse religions of mankind, if it is apprehended in as many different manners as there are different cultures, still the gift itself as distinct from its manifestations is transcultural.[30]

Lonergan's notion of transcultural communication offers some helpful insights for the work of the Church. It is necessary for the Church to take seriously the people to whom the message is communicated. He

---

[28] Ibid.
[29] Ibid.
[30] *Method*, 282-283.

maintains that Christian messengers must have right presuppositions, based on their own enlarged horizons. They should achieve an "intimate and accurate understanding of the culture and language of the people" with whom they are working. Every culture offers a context and resource for theology. Hence, the cultural resources must be used creatively.[31] For instance, in this age of efficient global communications, mass media should be used for the communication of the Gospel.

To apply the insights of Lonergan to the contemporary missiology would mean, first of all, that the transposition of the Christian message must take place in the linguistic and cultural contexts of the people. The anthropological insights that a missionary gains will render the communications relevant, effective, and enduring. One must understand what religions and doctrines are believed in the alien culture. No one can get an intimate understanding of the culture and language until one is able to identify with the people and their way of life. A bi-directional communication develops between the missionary and the host culture. One learns as one teaches.

No missionary should believe that the host culture is an enemy of the Gospel and, therefore, it is to be eliminated before the Gospel can take root in that culture. The host culture yields important insights and frameworks for the natural development of the message, and thus it offers support and stability for the Christian message. A missionary's intimate knowledge of the culture may further mean an appreciation for a way of life that is different from his or her own. Lonergan suggests that adaptation and a virtual grasping of the resources of the culture will make the transcultural communications natural and meaningful. Such resources may include ethnographic data, local languages, art, painting and other ingredients of culture that normally embody and convey meaning. These ingredients are vital to the theologian who is engaged in contextualizing theology in a given setting. Furthermore, other resources such as television, radio, internet, and film may be available to the Church. Knowledge and utilization of these resources help make proper and fuller use of the means of communications.

Preaching in a Pluralist Society

Lonergan speaks of three sources of pluralism. Preaching in a pluralist society means that the Church takes into consideration the manifold sources of pluralism such as the ones resulting from social, cultural, and

---

[31] Ibid., 362.

linguistic factors, or differentiated and undifferentiated consciousness or that resulting from the possibility of intellectual, moral, or religious conversion.[32] To preach the Gospel in any culture calls for a realization of the pluralism that exists in that culture. Lonergan reminds us that the Gospel must be preached to all nations, which means it should be preached to "every class in every culture in the manner that accords with the assimilative powers of that class and culture.[33] Communication of the Gospel should be as multiform as are the different common senses produced by the many languages, social forms, and cultural meanings. Preaching and teaching the message of the Gospel to every culture and nation may mean that the Church has to become all things to all men.[34] In order to communicate the Gospel in a way that makes sense to each brand of common sense, the preacher has to understand the message clearly. For Lonergan, using one's own cultural resources in preaching in another culture is not relevant communication. It is being "locked up" in one's own culture.[35]

Contextualization of theology must be encouraged against the attempts of transferring theology just as it has been developed in another cultural context. No human culture, according to Lonergan, is universal, normative, fixed, and immutable.[36]

Ecumenism and Dialogue as Communication

Ecumenism and dialogue, in Lonergan's view, can be considered as forms of communication. In the chapter on "Communications," he discusses the fruitfulness of these two forms of communication, especially in the context of the World Council of Christian Churches.[37] He understands the present-day ecumenical movement as a fruit of Christ's prayer for unity in John 17:21. The inner gift of God's love with the outer manifestation in Christ is the basis of Christian ecumenism.

Lonergan supports ecumenism in order to facilitate communication between people of different Christian traditions. There must be a greater unity among different Christian churches. The real unity is produced by

---

[32] Ibid.
[33] Ibid., 328.
[34] Ibid., 329.
[35] Ibid., 300.
[36] Ibid., xi.
[37] Ibid., 367.

the response to the one Lord in the one Spirit.³⁸ The Christian Church has many different denominations, and each of them has its doctrinal distinctives and polity. It is in the cognitive area that they differ from each other, but until the churches have a greater, common agreement, they should collaborate and fulfill the redemptive roles of the Christian Church in society. ³⁹ Ecumenical dialogue must take place among churches and among theologians of different traditions. Such collaborative efforts will prove to be advantageous for all churches, as they can help in the wise use of materials and human resources. Inter-church cooperation will result in the mutual edification of the churches and will increase the efficiency of their redemptive tasks in the world.

As another method of communication, Lonergan also proposes inter-religious dialogue, dialogue between Christians and representatives of other religions, based on the constitutive meaning of those religions. There is an urgent need for this type of communication in today's world, especially in light of the current interreligious conflicts and wars. God's gift of love and the religious experience of non-Christians should serve as a basis for interreligious dialog.⁴⁰

Religion is the "prior word" that God communicates to human beings. The question of God is raised in all cultures and religions. Moreover, there is a prior operation of the Holy Spirit in all religions, causing them to long for God, who is the supreme realization of self-transcendence. Also, there exists in every human being, what Lonergan calls "a region for the divine," "a shrine for ultimate holiness," and "a native orientation to the divine."⁴¹

The dialogue among Christian churches and between churches and other religions will create and promote mutual understanding. The church itself learns fresh lessons of conversion, as it learns from and through interreligious dialogues. Neither the Church nor its dialogue partner compromises its essential doctrines, but they learn from each other and are brought together to work for the common good of the society. The Church promotes its own meaning, but does not force it on others. Genuine dialogues can sharpen the redemptive focus of the Christian church and can help in the development and renewal of its ecclesiology.

---

³⁸ Ibid.
³⁹ Ibid., 368.
⁴⁰ Ibid., 119, 360.
⁴¹ Ibid., 103.

Concluding Critical Comments

As we have seen above, Bernard Lonergan's theological method gives rise to many interesting issues, such as the effective communication of the Gospel, contextualization of theology, cross-cultural communications in missions, unity of the Church, and the need for interreligious dialog in a pluralist society. All these issues must be addressed in the training programs of the Church and its educational institutions, so that the redemptive tasks of the Church in the world can be made more purposeful and effective. The insights that Lonergan provides in the area of transcultural communication of the Gospel are helpful guidelines for the missiological activities of the Church, in both Western and non-Westerm cultures. The task of developing a global perspective both in theological education and in the training programs of the Church and the seminary would broaden the outlook of future theologians, missiologists, and ministers who are called to communicate the Christian message in a shrinking global village.

Lonergan's notion of communications is well founded on an empirical understanding of culture that respects the values and meanings held by all human societies. He rightly insists on the efforts to Christian unity everywhere. This is particularly helpful and needed in countries where the Christian minority suffers persecution at the hand of the fundamentalist religious majority. The unity of all Christians is beneficial to the stability and continued ministry of the Church. Furthermore, the call for interreligious dialogue is relevant to the religio-cultural situations of the modern world because the relationship of Christianity to non-Christian religions has become a central theological issue in the present time.

BIBLIOGRAPHY

Primary Sources

Lonergan, Bernard J.F., *Method in Theology*, 2nd ed., United Kingdom: Darton Longman & Todd, 1972. Reprinted by University of Toronto Press, Toronto, 1990.

------*Insight: A Study of Human Understanding.* 3rd ed., New York: Philosophical Library, 1970.

Secondary Sources

Corcoran, Patrick, ed. *Looking at Lonergan's Method*, Dublin: Talbot Press, 1975.
Crowe, Frederick E. *The Lonergan Enterprise*, Cambridge, MA: Cowley Publications, 1980.
Crowe, Frederick E. *Method in Theology: An Organon for Our Tim*, Milwaukee, WI: Marquette University Press, 1980.
Mueller, J.J. *What Are They Saying About Theological Method?* NJ: Paulist Press, 1984.
Ormerod, Neil. *Method, Meaning and Revelation*, Lanham, MD: University Press of America, 2000.

Chapter Eight

J. Severino Croatto

The Use of the Exodus Motif in the Liberation Hermeneutic

Liberation theology[1] has been one of the most significant movements in the recent history of the church. It is generally understood to be a theology that has been worked out from the periphery, using those questions that are pertinent to the poor and the marginalized, but with global implications. As such, it invites praxis and calls for actions of liberation from a Gospel standpoint. The work of liberation that it espouses belongs to the contemporary history of the people, where they are oppressed.[2]

Latin America was the primary context in which was articulated this theology, which then gained currency in other cultures with similar life situations. As a theological movement with interdisciplinary concerns, liberation theology has facilitated the meeting of several academic areas, such as hermeneutics, epistemology, philosophy, ecclesiology, education, economics, and politics. Liberation theologians have challenged the way in which theology is articulated and practiced in the West. With the publication of a landmark book[3] by Gustavo Gutierrez, the Christian world began to think more critically about the theological concerns raised

---

[1] In fact, it is more accurate to speak of it in the plural because the movement has engendered several other contextually specific theologies on various continents. The earliest proponents were Gustavo Gutierrez, Juan Segundo, Jose Miranda, J. Severino Croatto, Clodovis Boff, and Jose Miguez-Bonino, who received inspiration from European political theology and the sociological concerns that it raised. These writers were critical of the ahistorical and socially disconnected way in which theology had been articulated in Europe. All of them, except the Methodist Miguez-Bonino, are from the Roman Catholic Church.
[2] Leonardo Boff and Clodovis Boff, *Introducing Liberation Theology* (Maryknoll, NY: Orbis Books, 1987), 88.
[3] Gustavo Gutierrez, *A Theology of Liberation: History, Politics, and Salvation* (Maryknoll, NY: Orbis Books, 1973).

by liberation theologians. From the 1970s to the present time, numerous volumes have been published on the subject of liberation. These writings fall into two major groups, namely, that which supports and defends the existing position and that which criticizes it and at the same time argues for a new approach.

The socio-politico-economic conditions that gave rise to liberation theologies continue to exist in both Latin America and other parts of the world, including Western societies, with little or no hope of social improvement. For example, in both the USA and Europe, various deep-seated problems arise from prolonged unemployment and deprivation of economic justice for the poor. The exploitation of people by multinational corporations is a subject of great concern in America, which has gaven rise to some popular protest movements in recent times. The socioeconomic situations in any country have a direct bearing on the life and work of the Church. The application of the Kingdom principles to the plight of the poor and the oppressed has been a key thought in the writings of J. Severino Croatto (1930-2004), who employed powerful biblical imagery to set forth his theological arguments.

J. Severino Croatto was an Argentinean Roman Catholic theologian whose primary fields of academic interest were the history and culture of the Ancient Near East, Classical Latin and Greek, Semitic languages and the phenomenology of religion, and biblical hermeneutics. Until his death in 2004, he was engaged in teaching as well as in popular education movements of Bible-reading in Spanish. His commitment to justice and peace for all, especially in the most difficult years of the military dictatorships in Latin America, has influenced many liberation theologians.

This chapter will discuss Croatto's use of the Exodus motif in the larger context of the liberation theological method. It will be shown that the common use of the *Exodus* motif in liberation hermeneutics is not without criticism. However, it is important for the church to listen to the concerns raised by Croatto and others like him. Their voices are still relevant to the Church's mission in the contemporary world.

The Nature and Task of Liberation Hermeneutics: Some General Observations

Certain major themes are common in the works of liberation theologians. *First* is a continuous reminder about the character of God's justice. God stands with the poor who have been denied justice. The work of the

Church is liberative, and it must be consistent with the character of a just God who demands justice for those who are oppressed and marginalized in the world. Being God's agent of liberation and healing in the world, the Church should raise awareness in the community about the plight of the poor. This responsibility calls for a conscious, liberative reading of the scriptures, followed by a social restructuring that would bring justice to the marginalized populations. Christian theology has largely ignored the plight of the people, so argue liberationists.

Second, liberation theology expresses a frustration with the classical European theology. This concern is discussed particularly in the works of Croatto, Gutierrez, Hanks, and Cone. James Cone, who is a proponent of Black theology, for instance, argues in his *God of the Oppressed*[4] that theology as articulated by white Americans was shaped by white sociopolitical interests. They interpreted the Gospel according to their own cultural and political interests, and their theologies have never transcended their interest groups. The theologians of this white persuasion have identified themselves with the dominant power structure of their time and failed to address the crucial socio-political issues outside their own cultural history.

In much the same way, Gutierrez criticizes the theology of the early centuries of the church for its contemplative life, which ignored the socio-political tasks in the society.[5] He argues that the theological discussions in Europe and America have been largely sterile academic affairs and have failed to give adequate attention to the realities of economic poverty and other social problems. Therefore, abstract theological talks, which do not seek to solve social problems, are not balanced.

Third, in its methodology, liberation theology proposes a "hermeneutical circle" that has four stages. *First*, one must have an ideological suspicion; that is, one should suspect perhaps there is something wrong in society, especially among the socially marginalized people. *Second*, using the sociological tools, one examines whether or not scripture justifies a situation and to what extent God's purposes in the world are fulfilled in it. *Third*, because of the bias in reading and understanding the Bible, one should entertain an "exegetical suspicion." This heightened suspicion is needed because the typical biased reading may have ignored the plight of the oppressed in the society. *Fourth*, the Church should have a pastoral response to the situation through concrete

---

[4] James H. Cone, *God of the Oppressed* (New York: The Seabury Press, 1975), 47.
[5] Gutierrez, 3, 4, 5.

actions that would bring help and liberation to the poor.[6] Theology informs praxis and praxis in turn helps one to look at theology again. But there is another important point: one has to start with the context, and not the biblical text. The reader approaches the text with the present experience as the starting point, and then, from the text he or she moves back to the present experience. The hermeneutical circle is seen as a new way of doing theology, which is aimed at establishing justice for the poor, which is an important task of the Gospel. This approach, which leads to what is popularly called the "preferential option for the poor," has received heavy criticisms from traditional theological circles.

In the *fourth* stage, liberation hermeneutics borrows Marxist tools for its social analysis, which is to aid in the reflection of that which is political in nature, and has invited vigorous criticisms from conservative Christians. It uses Marxist theory at the academic level and makes contact with Marxist groups at the practical level, because they cover common ground regarding the liberation of the poor and the oppressed.[7] Gutierrez points out that the social sciences are important tools for theological reflection in Latin America because the social, psychological, and biological sciences can aid in gaining a more complete understanding of the faith.[8] Theology can no longer stay detached from other human sciences, which could be quite consistent with the teachings of Jesus. For instance, a monastic trend characterized by a spiritual life, far removed from the concerns of the world, is no longer justifiable in a needy world.

This indifference is why all liberationists, including Croatto, have sharply criticized classical theology, which encouraged "charity" in the face of suffering, while giving no hope for changing the society, or even calling attention to the grace and power of God that are at work on behalf of the poor. Therefore, such theologies cannot be regarded as normative for other cultures.

Following the same line of argument, Clodovis Boff points out that in the interpretation of the scriptures, the new positivity of the human

---

[6] See for a helpful summary in Veli-Matti Kärkkäinen, *Christology: A Global Introduction* (Grand Rapids: Baker Academic, 2003), 225.
[7] See *Introducing Liberation Theology*, op. cit., p. 28, where the Boff brothers argue that "Marxism is never treated as a subject on its own but always *from and in relation to the poor*." It uses Marxism only as an *instrument* in its methodology. Emphasis original.
[8] Gutierrez, 4, 5.

sciences, which he calls the "socio-analytic mediation," is essential for moving the theological discourse into praxis.[9]

Still in the same context, the Boff brothers introduce three mediations in the hermeneutical task: socio-analytical (or historico-analytical) mediation, which operates in the world of the oppressed; hermeneutical mediation, which operates in the sphere of God's world; and practical mediation, which pertains to the sphere of action. They argue that these mediations provide help in probing the conditions of oppression in an effective way by trying to find out why the oppressed are oppressed and what God's plan is for the oppressed, and finally propose the course of action that is needed in the society.[10] The strongly-argued case for the pragmatic nature of theology is to address the cases of injustice in the world. The function of the Christian doctrine is to speak directly to such situations. Therefore, theology becomes critical reflection on praxis.[11]

The Exodus Motif in the Hermeneutics of Croatto

For hermeneutical reasons, certain books in the Bible are more favored than others for supporting liberation theology. The book of Exodus obviously is a preferred text because it recounts the religious and political liberation of the Hebrew slaves in Egypt. The Exodus event of the Old Testament becomes a celebrated case in liberation theology. Following Gutierrez and Hanks, Croatto speaks of the Exodus as a paradigm of oppression and liberation, which is fundamental to the interpretation of the revelation of God. The book reveals a God who is deeply concerned for the physical and spiritual wellbeing of his people. God's action in the story is mainly interpreted as a political action. In Croatto's view, liberating the Hebrews from the oppressive regime of Egypt and leading them into a land where they could form a new and more just society was God's plan for his people.

In *Exodus: A Hermeneutics of Freedom*,[12] Croatto sees the event as a central paradigm of God's liberating activity in history. It is a "salvific event" of great importance, not only in the life of the Hebrews but also in the lives of all who are similarly longing for liberation. The author

---

[9] Clodovis Boff, *Theology and Praxis*, trans. Robert R. Barr (New York: Orbis Books, 1987), 11.
[10] *Introducing Liberation Theology*, 24.
[11] Gutierrez, 6-15.
[12] *Exodus: A Hermeneutics of Freedom*, trans. Salvator Attanasio (New York: Orbis Books, 1978).

proposes a re-reading of the Exodus in the light of the experiences of the people of Latin America. Hermeneutics is not fixed in its final form forever, says Croatto. In other words, the Bible is not a "closed deposit" that has already "said it all."[13] Therefore, we must re-read the book of Exodus in order to bring out fresh meanings that are relevant to human situations. Because theology has to do with the quest for God, such a re-reading of the Word will help inform how to take hold of God in concrete human experiences. So, what Croatto claims to do in this work is to offer an epistemological tool for the hermeneutics of freedom. The Exodus event often is characterized as a type of redemption in Christ, and as such it is identified as one of the most important themes of the Bible. For the people of Latin America, this event is a "focal point of the first magnitude and an inexhaustible light."[14]

The key to Croatto's hermeneutics is the manner in which the biblical message wells up with salvific happenings and this, he believes, should be a presupposition for doing theology. Because God has not finished with human history and is still acting in it, theology must be "reformulated" to include the new manifestations of God in the contemporary history. The human events, for Croatto, are to be "deciphered as the locale of God's revelation."[15] This emphasis certainly is not a static understanding of the Bible, as there is a need for engaging the ongoing history of the world. Croatto's chief aim is to construct a theology of liberation that shows the relevance of the Bible in any given context and in any given time.[16] Indeed, the Bible is relevant to all human situations.

Redefining a Hermeneutic

The point of departure in Croatto's discussion is the liberation experience of the Hebrews. The method used is consistent with the hermeneutical circle explained above. Traditional theology starts with the exegesis of the text and its application to human situations. In Croatto's view, experiences, such as poverty and oppression, must serve as the starting point because of the conviction that the "facts must be, and are prior" to the interpretation of the Scripture.[17] Accordingly, the task is to create a

---

[13] *Biblical Hermeneutics*, trans. Robert Barr, (New York: Orbis Books, 1987), ix.
[14] Ibid., iv.
[15] Ibid., 5.
[16] Ibid., vi.
[17] Ibid., 11. This approach is common to most liberationists. For a similar discussion,

hermeneutical perspective for re-reading the scriptures on the basis of the experiences of oppression and poverty. He cautions that God is not "locked up" and moreover, He is not an object of mere intellectual exercise. The interpreter must see God speaking and acting continuously in history.

The book of Exodus, he argues, is a "reservoir of meaning," and as such, it offers promise of liberation to those who are oppressed. In *Biblical Hermeneutics*, Croatto first looks at the oppressive and alienating situation and experience of the people in Egypt.[18] The alienation had broken the spirit of the Hebrews. As a result, they were even "incapable of hoping for their salvation." This is why they refused to listen to Moses (Exodus 6:9). This peculiar situation of the Israelites is a "summit of human alienation when people no longer hope in their own liberation."[19] God's word to Moses (3:17) reveals his plan to liberate the people. This "conscienticizes" them. There are leaders in Latin America who can pronounce liberating and conscienticizing words.[20]

Furthermore, the book of Exodus reveals a "tension" and "dis-tension," as far as the experience of the people in Egypt is concerned. The tension is due to the fact that the Hebrews thought that their God had forgotten them, and dis-tension, because Yahweh remembered His promise. The book of Exodus offers a locus that is "characteristic, provocative, creative, inexhaustible, and kerygmatic."[21] Undoubtedly, it is the Exodus event that played a major role in the shaping of the history and the religious life of the people of Israel. Therefore, we must begin from this event. If we do not, neither Israel's faith nor the formation of its religious traditions and sacred books can be correctly understood.[22] It is a "radical datum." We see ourselves and our God in it.

Another point Croatto makes is that every human experience produces its "word" and "meaning." The meaning of the event has efficacy to trigger other experiences or situations. Meaning produced by an event can be manifested in other events. The first event thus can be called the "originary" or "founding" event. The Exodus was an originary event and

---

see Juan Segundo, *The Liberation of Theology*, trans. J. Drury (Dublin: Gill & Macmillan), 1977, 7-8.

[18] A similar argument is found in Gutierrez, where he highlights the repression, alienating work, and the enforced birth control policy of Egypt, p. 156.

[19] Ibid., 17.

[20] Ibid., 28.

[21] Ibid., 12.

[22] Ibid.

as such, it now manifests a "meaning surplus."[23] Thus, an event does not show all its latent meanings and decisive characteristics right at the time it occurs. Our personal experiences, likewise, are full of meanings, all of which do not manifest right when they occur. Each one has a hidden depth from which arise newer aspects of meanings, as time goes by. Hence, the Hebrew experience can speak afresh to us because it acquires new and deeper meanings even a long time after it has taken place.

The conviction that a human event does not exhaust itself simply by occurring is central to Croatto's argument. Here, he draws upon H. G. Gadamer's "historical effect." Thus, one can say that the human events have the capacity to generate new events. The meaning of the more recent event is found to be already included within the prior event. This, I think, is an interesting observation either in the re-reading of a particular text, or in the case of any event that we witness today. Take for example, the "Arab uprising" in the Middle East. The meaning that constituted the movement in one country has inspired and triggered similar movements in other parts of the Middle East and Europe. To use a maxim from Bernard Lonergan, "situations are the cumulative product of previous actions."[24] Accordingly, each situation has meaning, and that meaning is communicative.

A Framework for Hermeneutics

In *Biblical Hermeneutics*, Croatto sets forth a theoretical framework. He recognizes a tension between a "fixed text," which is from an alien cultural milieu, and a "living word," which is capable of forging history. The solution to this tension is a "fertile re-reading" of the text.[25] The interpretive phenomenon is "omnipresent," and it requires what Croatto calls the "theoretical instrumentation," which enables us to re-read the text in such a way that we can tap its "reservoir of meaning".[26] This instrumentation is especially an aid to those for whom the Bible appears to be a sort of puzzle, rather than a clear message.

Croatto acknowledges several approaches to the interpretation of the Bible. The Bible is both a *Sprachreignis* (language event) and a *Wortereignis* (word event), and neither of these can exhaust the Bible. Therefore, in order to capture the wealth and methodological value in its totality, we

---

[23] *Biblical Hermeneutics*, 37.
[24] Lonergan, 358.
[25] Ibid., ix.
[26] Ibid., 10.

should approach hermeneutics by way of the sciences of language.[27] Events are gathered up in language, which needs to be interpreted. Because of the importance of the sciences of language, hermeneutics must, first of all, be situated on the semiotics, the science of signs, the most comprehensive expression of which is language in the strict sense. He further argues that both hermeneutics and semiotics must have reading of the text as a production of meaning, and not a repetition of meaning.

The meaning of the text is vital to the present reality of oppression and, therefore, the Bible should not be read from a "historicist" perspective because the facts in that case will be read as if they had occurred only in the way in which they are recounted and thus rob them of hermeneutic distance that has restructured their meaning. An originary event such as the Exodus will broaden its meaning when it is read at a distance. It will incorporate new events such as the crossing of the Jordan, which was "retrojected" to the crossing of the Red sea. The Exodus as a founding event "overspills" with signification on to the appropriation of the Promised Land. This reading unites the events of the originary liberation from Egypt and the present occupation of the land. The Exodus as an originary event has a "memory," which the Bible keeps on re-presenting in every literary genre and in every age. This re-presentation is not a repetition of the meaning but a scanning of the reservoir of meanings.[28]

The originary events that led to the formation of the new people of God are not exhausted in their first narration. Rather, they "enlarge" in meaning by way of their projections into the life of the people. In order to express this "meaning surplus," the "word" of the event "redimensions" and reworks the event. The originary event was also a "referent" for the Hebrews in their later years, as they went back to it in order to recapture its hope when they fell into the hand of the oppressors. Their liberation event in Egypt had a foundational character, and its meaning is generated by means of a "causal linkage" or by way of interpretation. The return from the Babylonian captivity was interpreted as a new exodus.[29] The exodus event thus presents us with a deeper dimension of signification and an inexhaustibility of its inspiration and meaning for today.

---

[27] Ibid., 10.
[28] Ibid., 8.
[29] Isaiah 11:15,16; 19:16-25; 43:16-21; 51:9-11. See Ibid., p. 39.

The Exodus Event As Political Liberation

Croatto sees in the liberating event of the Exodus high political and social significance. In speaking of the oppressive conditions in which the Hebrews lived, Croatto points out:

> The oppression in Egypt is of political order because it is the authority of the Pharaoh that exploits a group in his country, an alien ethnic minority to boot. The oppression is exercised from the seat of political power. It was also a way of getting rid of the hated Asiatics, as we know from the Egyptian texts.[30]

The book of Exodus speaks much about the work of God on behalf of his people, who groan under their oppressive burden. The liberationists prefer a socio-political interpretation to any other approach. For example, Gutierrez, in his *A Theology of Liberation*, depicts the Exodus event as a political action of breaking away from a situation of despoliation for the construction of a just and fraternal society. For him, the Exodus event is a political liberation through which Yahweh's love for his people is expressed.[31] Reducing an event or concept to some of its aspects is not an uncommon trend in liberation theology.[32]

There are political issues in the book of Exodus, such as the multiplication of the aliens, which must have posed a serious political threat to the Egyptians. Furthermore, the appointment of oppressive taskmasters and the order to annihilate the male Israelite children might have resulted from a fear of the foreigners and the potential danger they might one day pose to the internal security of the nation. Croatto, like Gutierrez, characterizes the exodus event as a socio-political liberation. He says that "God began the process of liberation not by forgiving personal sins but by physical-social liberation".[33] He stresses that

---

[30] *Exodus*, 18.
[31] Gutierrez, 157.
[32] Rosemary R. Ruether, *Women-Church* (San Francisco: Harper & Row, 1985) is very much patterned after Liberation theology language. She defines the Church, not in its totality, including biblical and theological dimensions, but in its social and political dimensions. She has already justified this bias because her perspective is that of a religious feminist who seeks to reclaim "aspects of the biblical tradition" and who also sees the need "to go back behind biblical religion and transcend it," 25, 34.
[33] *Exodus*, 18.

God did not begin saving in the spiritual order, not even from sin. God saves total human beings whose human fulfillment can be impeded not only by themselves (sin) but also by other human beings who abuse their power or their social status. This observation has grave hermeneutical consequences for a Latin American or Third World re-reading of the message of the Exodus event. Have we paid sufficient attention to the fact that the first, exemplary liberation event, which "reveals" the God of salvation, was political and social?[34]

Croatto's emphasis on the political aspect of the Exodus event must be examined carefully. He, like his colleagues, has a strong conviction that the Bible is applicable to the present reality of life and that theology needs natural and human sciences to understand the multidimensional character of the Christian faith. Doing theology from the perspective of the poor of the Latin America is commendable. However, Exodus is not all political, and the political reality is only one of the several dimensions or aspects that are integrally related to its other aspects. Croatto's approach makes the equally important biblical and theological questions fall into secondary importance.

Some of the theological concerns in the book of Exodus are the recognition of Yahweh as God,[35] the ultimate aim of the miracles performed in Egypt, the wrath of God against the unbelieving, and God's protection for those who seek refuge in him.[36] The event has ensuing theological significance, as they are clearly manifested in the entire history of Israel and the teaching of its religious institutions such as the Passover, Sabbatical year, the Sabbath and the Jubilee year. The freedom from slavery that came as a result of God's act of love did, in fact, help in the formation of a new community. But it was not one guided by any political or democratic ideals. The Exodus community was shaped by God's will. Paul L. Schrieber who has this to say about the religious significance and the ultimate goal of the Exodus:

> Yahweh redeemed Israel so they might serve Him instead of Pharaoh. The outcome and sign of the change in master was that Israel served Yahweh at Mount Sinai (Ex.3:12). This means that the Israelites, freed from the slavery of Egypt, were now His servants, who lived under His direction and protection regardless

---

[34] Ibid.
[35] Exod. 5:2
[36] Exod. 12:12

of their social status (Lev.25:42, 55). Once again, the theological, theocratic dimensions come to the fore.[37]

This theological significance does not negate the political reality of a liberated community. However, one must recognize that in biblical theology, the Exodus event is a `type' of salvation that found its fulfilment in Jesus Christ. Thus, the book of Exodus offers us a great reservoir of redemptive themes and languages that no exegete can ignore (Ex. 12:42, 15; cf. Dt. 15, 16; Rev. 15:3).

Furthermore, one should also view the Exodus in the light of the Abrahamic covenant. Exodus 2:24 says: "God heard their groaning and he remembered his covenant with Abraham, Isaac and Jacob. So God looked on the Israelites and was concerned about them." This divine remembering and concern may be traced back to the original promise to Abraham: "In the fourth generation your descendants will come back here, for the sin of the Amorites has not reached its full measure."[38]

The scripture confirms that the Exodus event was a fulfilment of the divine promise and, therefore, it was not an act that suddenly sprang up because of the people's cry of oppression. Further, the Exodus event was not initiated by the Hebrews, as some seem to think. The Bible offers us no proof that the liberation event was the work of their own hands, or even the outcome of any sociopolitical tactic that they had devised. They neither had planned to overthrow Pharaoh nor had resorted to violence against their oppressors. This is not to suggest that the oppressed should patiently suffer oppression or that they should not resist the oppressor and overcome the unjust laws through just means. Rather, it suggests that the liberation in the Exodus must be understood in the context of the sovereign power of God, who was concerned about the total well-being of his people.

The Question of Reductionism and Ideology

A serious criticism that can be directed against liberation theologians is that their method is reductive, meaning that theology, which has many dimensions, is reduced to merely some political or sociological aspect. Furthermore, a theology is considered to be reductive when it does not intend to reproduce the entire theological system that has been handed

---

[37] Paul L. Schrieber, "Liberation Theology and the Old Testament: An Exegetical Critique," *Concordia Journal* 13 (1987): 33.
[38] Gen. 15:15, quoted by Schrieber

down by tradition.[39] Reductionism fails to take account of the complete story of the Bible, ignoring its integral inter-relatedness. The reductionistic tendency produces what Bernard Lonergan calls, a "mutilated and distorted view."[40]

Theology, as a reflection on the Bible and as a systematized study of the revelation of God, reveals the manifold attributes of God. As a science, it seeks to present the various aspects of God and humanity. The Bible, for example, reveals not only the redemptive but also the social, political, lingual, economic, and aesthetic aspects of life. Therefore, no approach should reduce the Bible to only one of these aspects as an absolute. The analysis of any one of these aspects should be done in the larger context of the whole of scripture. Reducing reality to one aspect betrays the indissoluble cohesion of God's creation and destroys the wholeness of meaning.[41]

Croatto's understanding of the Exodus as a "reservoir of meaning" is correct. However, it should be remembered that this meaning is not merely political. A balanced and justifiable hermeneutic considers each aspect of the Exodus in relation to the entire redemptive story of the Bible. One may uncover moments of truth in each of the aspects but interpreting these moments of truth as a view of the totality of reality is erroneous and can be interpreted as coming from an idolatrous understanding of reality, which is present at the root of ideology.[42] In its original sense, ideology means an entire system of values, conceptions, convictions, and norms that are used as a set of tools for reaching a single concrete, all-encompassing societal end.[43] Reductionism and ideology are related to each other. Ideology, understood in a positive sense, is related to praxis and is a necessary component of the liberation hermeneutics.

---

[39] See Juan L. Segundo's *A Theology for the Artisans of a New Humanity*, Vol. 1, trans. John Drury (Maryknoll, NY: Orbis Books, 1973), ix.
[40] Ibid., 248.
[41] I am indebted to Herman Dooyeweerd for this principle. See his *Roots of Western Culture: Pagan, Secular and Christian Options*, trans. John Kraay, (Toronto: Wedge Publishing Foundation, 1979), 40, 41.
[42] Ibid., 41. Here the term 'Ideology' is used in the negative sense. A positive use of the term is found in Segundo's *The Liberation of Theology*, p. 181, where ideology is needed as a motivation for action.
[43] See Bob Goudzwaard, *Idols of Our Time* (Illinois: IV Press, 1981), 18-24. Goudzwaard states that each ideology started as a legitimate goal and that when a goal is overtly pursued beyond all limits it develops into an ideology and that an idolatrous ground motive is present at the root of every ideology. It is hard to determine at what point a legitimate goal ends and an ideology begins.

The Question of God Taking Sides with the Poor

Croatto points out that Jesus carried out his liberation "on the basis of his identification with the poor" and that he was "in solidarity with the poor as one of them".[44] He also says that it is in the process of liberation that we understand God as the Saviour. The words of Jesus had profound impacts upon the poor of his days, as they were "contextual and conscienticizing," which enabled the poor and the oppressed to rise from the obscurity of their "being less" to their "being more." Jesus cleared their path, which was obstructed by tradition and other oppressive structures. He liberated the oppressed by creating a "new person" in them, and His activity paved the way so that the "human being can emerge."[45]

Although these significant expressions serve the liberation paradigm, especially from the vantage point of the Kingdom of God, the liberation maxim of the `preferential option for the poor' can be seen as a challenge to the Old Testament exegesis. Is it biblically correct to say that God takes sides with the poor individual, regardless of whether that person is godly or ungodly?

The Bible reveals God as a God of justice, which means that all are equal before him. He is the *summum bonum*, the highest good for all of them. His benevolent interest is not restricted to believers; they only appreciate it better and use its blessings for His service. God does not withdraw his love completely from the sinner (because the person still bears the image of God), and at the same time he loves those who are in Christ with a special love (John 3:16; Matt. 5: 44-45; John 16:27; Rom. 5:8; 1 John 3:1). He is merciful to the poor and the oppressed. However, the mercy of God is not opposed to his justice. This perfection of God manifests itself especially in giving every person his or her due. The violation of justice in his created order is an offence against His nature and will. From this perspective, one can clearly see why oppression of the poor is a violation of God's principle of justice and why God takes a special interest in their welfare.

However, we should also realize that the poor can equally be guilty of violating the principle of justice if they resort to violence against the rich or other poor. God does not approve of such cases of injustice, no matter who the perpetrator is. The ultimate standard of judgment is God's own righteousness, and not the socio-economic status of the individual person.

---

[44] *Exodus*, 51.
[45] Ibid., 27, 45, 51.

The liberation hermeneutic does not make a distinction between the poor who are righteous and the poor who are wicked. In a serious issue such as this one, we should base our hermeneutical method, first of all, on what a person *is* (i.e., his or her relationship with God in Christ) and not on what a person *has* (i.e., possession, or poverty). This means that the liberation methodology should not overstate its case. Rather it should define and clarify its language and concepts more clearly.

God is, indeed, concerned about the poor and their state of suffering, and equally true is that He does not hate the rich who honour Him with their lives and resources. And in fact, the Bible has enough to teach us that the wealth acquired through just and godly means can be a sign of God's favour (Deut. 8). It is a truth that the poor may be as wicked as the rich (Jer. 5:1-3). Moreover, poverty may result from one's own negligence in life (Prov.10:4, 14:23; 13:18).

Thomas D. Hanks, a Costa Rican theologian briefly discusses some twenty causes of poverty found in the Old Testament.[46] According to him, by far the majority of the texts that suggest causes for poverty refer to oppression. Hanks sees oppression as a fundamental category of biblical theology. Although he is right in criticizing the classical theologies[47] for neglecting this theme, he does not make it clear whether people are poor because of the prevailing oppression, or they are oppressed because of their poverty.

The concept of the 'poor' as used in liberation theology draws a lot of criticisms.[48] For example, Paul Schrieber observes that the work of deliverance of the oppressed is tied explicitly to the forgiveness of sins in the context of the history of salvation of Yahweh's covenant people.[49] According to him, liberation theologians use terms such as "poor", "rich" and "oppressed" in such a way as to be "transmogrified beyond recognition in the Biblical context".[50] Schrieber's critique in this context is interesting:

> The broader dimensions of these terms become evident in considering words used in context and parallel. The poor and needy are identified as those who love Yahweh, who trust in Him, who seek Him, who are faithful, who are His servants, who

---

[46] Thomas D. Hanks, *God So Loved The Third World: The Bible, The Reformation, and Liberation Theologies*, (Maryknoll, NY: Orbis Books, 1983).
[47] Ibid, 38.
[48] Ibid.,
[49] Ibid., 39.
[50] Ibid., 38.

are upright and righteous who love His name and call on it, and who await the Messiah (Pss. 12; 140:12-13; 40:17; 49:9-10; 69:22,35,36, 116:3-11; 22:23, Zeph. 3:12-13). Conversely, those who oppress the poor are not simply the rich upper class but are the wicked, haters, persecutors, despoilers, arrogant, violent, and those who devise evil (Pss. 35:4; 9:17;10:4; 12:8; 94; 140:5, 9:22).[51]

The Liberation Methods in Conflict

Finally, Croatto's use of the Exodus paradigm comes in sharp conflict with other liberation theologies, specifically the Palestinian liberation theology. Naim Stifan Ateek warns against the abuse of the Exodus. He sees the paradigm as unsuitable for those who look for a Palestinian liberation theology. In his book *Justice and Only Justice*,[52] Ateek argues that the message of the Exodus is very much abused by both religious Zionists and the Christian fundamentalists who see in it a call for the physical return of the Jews to the land, rendering it difficult for the Palestinians to appreciate it. [53] While refuting the need for re-reading the Exodus with the liberationist's aims, Ateek has this objection to offer:

> For the Jews who came to establish the State of Israel, their journey to Palestine was an exodus from the different nations where they had been living and a return to the Promised Land. Obviously, for them, the imagery has connected the ancient past and the present. This uncritical transposition, however, makes the Palestinians appear to represent the old Canaanites who were in the land at the time and who at God's command needed to be dispossessed. The Exodus and the conquest of Canaan are, in the minds of many people, a unified and inseparable theme. For to need an exodus, one must have promised land. To choose the motif of conquest of the Promised Land is to invite the need for the oppression, assimilation, control, or dispossession of the indigenous population.[54]

---

[51]Ibid., 39.
[52] Naim Stifan Ateek, *Justice and Only Justice*. (Maryknoll, NY: Orbis Books, 1989). This book proposes a Palestinian theology of liberation.
[53] Ibid., 87.
[54]Ibid.

Concluding Critical Comments

The concerns of liberation theology with respect to addressing poverty and injustice are legitimate. They come as a challenge to the moral indifference of the Church that fails to act in solidarity with the poor and the oppressed. The Church must apply the meaning of the Christian faith to the whole of the society. Instead of unnecessarily restricting the full import of the Gospel to personal life by spiritualizing and personalizing it, the Church must extend it to social situations, where the poor and the oppressed suffer under the heavy hands of oppressors. Theologians can examine critically the art of social analysis carried out in ideologically-based movements such as Marxism, but there is no pressing need for borrowing such analytical framework, as they do not recognize the claims of Jesus. In fact, Christian theologians can be more thoroughgoing and effective than others in dealing with the spiritual and social problems of the people. Hence, theological thinking must emerge from the intellectual world of the elites to the concrete world of the oppressed.

Croatto is right in showing that our doctrines such as `Sin' and `Salvation' are applied not only to personal life but also to social and political structures, which have been permeated by sin. Exposing their sinfulness and correcting the situation is an important Christian task. The Church must not obstruct justice; rather, it must lead the way to establishing justice for all. For this task, the Church must encourage and practice internal critique, knowing that without it, it cannot bring critique to the unjust world outside.

Croatto, like other liberation theologians, shows how `theology' and `praxis' are related to each other in the exegesis of the Bible. Theology must be practical, not relegated to the inner recesses of the soul. The re-reading of the Exodus does make the work of the exegete relevant. The purpose of this re-reading should be to learn more and more about what the scripture says about human situations, and not to change the text and its original message.

Every nation struggles with the problems of unequal economic status, dehumanizing poverty and injustice, which are situations deplored by prophets. Just as the divine justice has a multidimensional character, so the work of the Church must also be multidimensional in character. The notion of justice embraces the whole spectrum of ethical and social values.

The Old Testament term *zedeqah*, which is translated *righteousness* or *justice*, reveals the all-encompassing nature of the Christian faith and practice. Croatto emphasizes the concept with all the seriousness that it needs. Amos, the prophet of social justice, points out that worship and praise are not acceptable to God, unless justice "rolls down like waters and righteousness like an ever-flowing stream." God is certainly concerned about the poor and the exploited. The Church must stand in solidarity with them so that, as Croatto says, "the human being can emerge." Christ's offer of salvation is linked with the freedom that characterizes the human existence here and now. The meanings of salvation must come to bear upon liberation and humanization, and, therefore, as Croatto says, as human individuals, who are also political beings, the Church must work toward establishing God's Kingdom here and now.

Liberation hermeneutics should also be seen as a challenge to our way of doing mission in a politically oppressed and economically poor world. Croatto draws our attention to the social relevance of the Christian faith. To use Jürgen Moltmann's language, the hope of the Gospel has a polemic and liberating relation, not only to the religions and ideologies of men, but still more to the factual, political life of the person and to the relationships in which this life is lived.[55] The Christian mission to the world must be informed by the cross of Christ, lest it becomes a mere sociological crusade.

Finally, the issue of poverty is not limited to the Third World. Western nations, including America, also have their own poor and oppressed. The problems of racial segregation, slavery, and poverty in American history are subjects of liberation theology. The churches are not always and everywhere known for fairness, racial tolerance, and equity. In fact, based on the numerous case studies and reports, one could argue that these issues are as much a problem in churches as elsewhere. Many of these churches have given unconditional support to ideologically-motivated governments to wage wars upon the peoples around the world, which have resulted in massacres, perpetuation of poverty and homelessness, and destabilization of peoples around the world. The much-needed liberation for the economically poor and socially marginalized in the Global South is not only from their own domestic patterns and forces of oppression, but also from those imposed upon them by other nations, which have been responsible for sustaining or creating patterns of oppression. The concerns and voices of liberation theologians are relevant, even in the West, where people suffer despoliation and injustice under the hands of more powerful people or structures.

---

[55] Jürgen Moltmann, *Theology of Hope* (London: SCM Press, 1967), 329-30.

The questions raised by liberation theologians in matters of hermeneutics, preaching, praxis, mission, and concern for the poor are crucial for theological education. They are the contexts in which pastors and missionaries work. The effectiveness of the missionaries and pastors depend upon how they apply the interpreted texts to the concrete realities of the people. And in terms of theological education, no college or seminary can be relevant to its cultural context without addressing the plight of humanity in its own neighbourhood. In both hemispheres of the world, economic poverty and social injustice are prevalent. Liberation theologians have been successful in drawing our attention to these crucial problems.

BIBLIOGRAPHY

Books

Ateek, Naim Stifan. *Justice and Justice Only: A Palestinian Theology of Liberation*, Maryknoll, New York: Orbis Books, 1989.
Belli, Humberto and Ronald Nash. *Beyond Liberation Theology*, Grand Rapids: Baker House, 1992.
Boff, Leonardo. *Ecclesiogenesis: The Base Communities Reinvent the Church*, Maryknoll, NY: Orbis, 1986.
------*Jesus Christ Liberator*, Maryknoll, NY: Orbis Books, 1978.
Boff, Lenardo and Clodovis Boff. *Introducing Liberation Theology*, trans. Paul Burns, Maryknoll, NY: Orbis Books, 1987.
Bonino, Jose Miguez. *Room to Be People*. Philadelphia: Fortress Press, 1979.
Cone, James H. *A Black Theology of Liberation*, 2nd ed., Maryknoll, NY.: OrbisBooks, 1986.
------*God of the Oppressed*, Maryknoll, NY: Orbis, 1997.
Croatto, J. Severino. *Exodus: A Hermeneutics of Freedom*, trans. Salvator Attanasio, Maryknoll, NY: Orbis Books, 1981.
------*Biblical Hermeneutics: Toward a Theory of Reading as the Production of Meaning*, trans. Robert R. Barr. Maryknoll, NY: Orbis Books, 1987.
Dooyeweerd, Herman, *The Roots of Western Culture: Pagan, Secular, and Christian Options*, trans. John Kraay, Toronto: Wedge Publishing Foundations, 1979.
----------. *Biblical Hermeneutics*, trans. Robert R. Barr, Maryknoll, NY: Orbis Books, 1987.
Goudzwaard, Bob. *Idols of Our Time*, Illinois: IV Press, 1981.
Gutierrez, Gustavo. *A Theology of Liberation*, translated and edited by Sister Caridad Inda and John Eagleson, New York: Orbis Books, 1971.
Hanks, Thomas D. *God So Loved The Third World*, trans. James C. Dekker, Maryknoll, NY: Orbis Books, 1983.
Haight, Roger. *An Alternative Vision: An Interpretation of Liberation Theology*. New York: Paulist Press, 1985.
Käarkkäinen, Veli-Matti. *Christology: A Global Introduction*. Grand Rapids, MI: Baker Academic, 2003.
Kirk, Andrew J. *Liberation Theology: An Evangelical View From the Third World*, London: Marshall Morgan & Scott, 1979.
Marshall, Paul. *Thine Is The Kingdom*, London: Marshall Morgan & Scott, 1984.
McGovern, Arthur F. *Liberation Theology and Its Critics: Toward and Assessment*, New York: Orbis Books, 1989.
Moltmann, Jürgen. *Theology of Hope*. London: SCM Press, 1967.
Pope-Levison, Priscilla and John R. Levison. *Return to Babel: Global Perspectives on the Bible*, Louisville, KY: Westminster John Knox Press, 1999.

Articles

Preus, J. A. O. "Liberation Theology: Basic Themes and Methodology," *Concordia Journal,* Vol. 13, No.1, 1987.

Schrieber, Paul L. "Liberation Theology and the Old Testament: An Exegetical Critique," *Concordia Journal,* Vol. 13, No. 1, 1987.

Wells, Harold G. "The Question of Ideological Determination in Liberation Theology," *Toronto Journal of Theology,* Vol. 3, No. 2, 1987.

Chapter Nine

Lesslie Newbigin

The Concept of 'Religion' and Salvation of Non-Christians

A prominent ecumenical theologian of the late 20th century, Lesslie Newbigin (1909-1998) received much attention among Christians of all persuasions across the globe. His work *The Household of God*[1] had been said to have influenced the writing of *Lumen Gentium*. In 1947, he was elected to be one of the CSI bishops in Madura and Ramnad, and then a leader in the World Council of Churches. His writings have been a reference point for many contemporary theologians and ministers. Several theological seminaries in Europe and North America have adopted his works for their ministerial programs. His concern has been to interpret the Gospel afresh in the changing religio-cultural situations of the world.

Newbigin's debate with pluralist theologians is well documented elsewhere. [2] The works of these theologians, who challenge the uniqueness of the Christian revelation by advocating the salvific nature of non-Christian religions, have made inroads into some major Christian denominations.

The purpose of this chapter is to examine Newbigin's concept of religion, especially in relation to Hinduism and other non-Christian religions, which some theologians say are salvific. Some pluralist theologians have proposed various models for the unity of all religions, the claims of which are examined by Newbigin in some of his later writings. This inquiry into the salvific nature of religions would also lead

---

[1] *The Household of God* (London: SCM Press, 1953). This classic work about the nature of Church has been translated into several major languages. Newbigin narrates its impact upon the Christian churches in his *Unfinished Agenda: An Autobiography* (Grand Rapids: Eerdmans, 1985), 136 -137.
[2] For a detailed presentation of the debate between Newbigin and the pluralist theologians, see J. M. Thomas, *Christ and the World of Religions: Lesslie Newbigin's Theology* (Carrollton, Texas: Ekklesia Society Publication, 2011), Ch. 4.

us to consider some aspects of Newbigin's view of Christ and the salvation of non-Christians.

Newbigin and the Concept of 'Religion'

Newbigin's experience of Hinduism began in Kanchipuram, one of the most sacred Hindu cities in India. His exposure to the Vedanta and its profoundly rational worldview prepared him to be a foremost interpreter of Hinduism and its implications for the ministry of the Christian church. For our present purpose, some of his writings[3] are more important than the others. The study of the *Svetasvara Upanishad* and the Gospel of John with the Swami of the Ramakrishna Mission had a great influence on his view of non-Christian religions. For Newbigin, the salvific nature of a religion cannot be determined, unless we understand what is meant by the word 'religion.'

The word *religion* is a very complex one to define; in fact, it is a "notoriously difficult" term, which needs to be probed thoroughly.[4] *First*, it can be used to describe any system of belief and practice that entails some sort of transcendence of the experience of the senses. In this sense, it is too vague to be useful. *Second*, it is used to refer to beliefs and practices concerning God and the immortal soul, in which case it is too narrow, because it excludes the original nontheistic teachings of the Buddha. Newbigin himself uses this word "to refer to that which has final authority for a believer or a society, both in the sense that it determines his scale of values and in the sense that it provides the models, the basic patterns through which the believer grasps and organizes his experience."[5] When used in this way, the word will include both ideologies and religions. But there are also cases in which what a person calls his or her religion may in fact be other than the ultimately authoritative factor in his or her thinking and acting. Accordingly, one may be called a Christian and yet limit the operation of the Christian commitment to a restricted area of his or her life and the ultimate commitment could be to some other way of living. In such cases, the commitment to Christ will be conditioned by one's commitment to the other way of living, and the latter will be the real religion.

---

[3] *The Finality of Christ* (London: SCM Press, 1969), *The Open Secret* (Grand Rapids: Eerdmans, 1978), and *The Gospel in a Pluralist Society* (Grand Rapids: Eerdmans, 1989). All of them engage the concerns of religious pluralism.
[4] *Open Secret*, 181.
[5] Ibid., 182.

Religionswissenschaft, ⁶ the "increasingly prestigious academic discipline," is of no use to Newbigin, because he is more concerned with the issues arising from the encounter of different and discordant religious commitments, which are the ultimate commitments of the people.[7]

Because the word *religion* has a range of meanings, one must study the meanings closely. The major religions can be placed in three groups.[8] The first group (Judaism, Christianity, and Islam) understands God's self-revelation in historical terms. Here, one must distinguish among them because the Jews are waiting for a Messiah still to come, Christians believe that Jesus is the Messiah, and Islam does not believe in a Messiah but in a succession of prophets culminating in Muhammad. The second group is composed of Indian religions, which are 'a-historical' with respect to the essential religious experience. The third group is based on worldviews, namely, the atomic, the oceanic, and the relational. The atomic view is characteristic of the modern Western society, which sees reality in terms of its autonomous individual unit, the ultimate constituent of society. The oceanic view sees all things as ultimately merged into one entity as proposed by Hinduism - Atman is Brahman. The third relational view sees everything as constituted by relationships, whether the material world or human society. This view is also shared by the so-called primal religions.[9]

By turning to this complex analysis of religions, Newbigin is proving his point that when we use the word *religion*, we are making several assumptions that need to be questioned and clearly examined before determining their salvific nature. His theological opponents, who propose the unity of all religious traditions and their salvific nature, have ignored the discordant makeup of these religions.

Furthermore, separating religion and culture is difficult; they are integrally related. Religion is not a separate activity set apart from the rest of life,[10] which increases the complexity of its precise interpretation. No pluralist theologian recognizes this inseparable link between the two. In fact, Clifford Geertz [11] has the same position as Newbigin on the

---

[6] Here, Newbigin disagrees with the approach to religions on the basis of scientific method, as proposed by Max Müller, because the very foundation of science might be questioned by one of these religions so studied.
[7] Ibid.
[8] *Gospel*, 171-72.
[9] Ibid., 172.
[10] Ibid.
[11] Clifford Geertz, "Religion as a Cultural System," *The Interpretation of Cultures* (New York: Basic Books, 1973), 119, 124.

sociological nature of religions. Religion dictates social order to a great extent, a reality that is so evident, for example, in the social life of India. There, life is influenced by the beliefs and practices of Hinduism. Thus, the whole cultural life of the society is permeated by beliefs, and what we call *religion* is a "whole world view, a way of understanding the whole of human experience."[12]

Such an integral worldview, typical of India, is quite different from that of the post-Enlightenment Western societies, where there exists a dichotomy between the 'sacred affairs' and the `secular affairs'.[13] The point that Newbigin stresses here is not only about the complexity of the word *religion*, but also the unspoken assumption in the contemporary debate about Christianity and the world religions, where this word is limited to mean the `primary medium of human contact with the divine'. This assumption needs to be challenged.[14] Although a personal element exists in every religion, the major religions of the world, such as Hinduism and Islam, have been great social powers. As J. H. Bavinck puts it, human beings "act collectively, especially when they respond to what is called the deepest realities of life."[15]

Thus, the word *religion* cannot be extricated easily from the cultural realities, and in Newbigin's thought, the concept of religious plurality is a "subset of cultural plurality."[16] Therefore, any understanding of salvation in this respect has to do with the complex phenomenon of religion and its inseparable matrix called culture.

A Critical Examination of Christian Attitudes to Other Religions

Newbigin examines a number of traditional Christian attitudes towards non-Christian religions.

---

[12] *Gospel*, 172.
[13] Ibid.
[14] Ibid.
[15] J. H. Bavinck, *The Church Between Temple and Mosque: A Study of the Relationship Between The Christian Faith and Other Religions* (Grand Rapids: Eerdmans, 1967), 19.
[16] See George Hunsberger, *Bearing the Witness of the Spirit* (Grand Rapids: Eerdmans, 1998), 198, for an exposition of this religion-culture link and the limitations of the concept of religion in Newbigin.

"Non-Christian Religions as false"

Newbigin shows no outright rejection of these religions as being false and devoid of any moral values. Rather, they contain "abundant spiritual fruits." But, when the Gospel of John speaks of the light that lightens every man, it is not referring to the non-Christian religions as the revealer of this light. At the same time, "it is impossible for the Christian to say that those outside the church are totally devoid of the truth."[17] But Newbigin, who has witnessed certain evil manifestations of Hinduism, thinks that *religion* can be the "primary area of darkness." When the New Testament affirms that God has nowhere left Himself without a witness, it does not say that this witness is to be found in the sphere of what we call religion.

"Non-Christian Religions as works of the Devil"

This attitude, typical of Justin Martyr as found in his *Apology*, characterizes non-Christian religions as the work of the devil and, therefore, their similarities to Christianity are attributed to demonic cunning. However, pagan philosophy may carry some light of the Logos. Newbigin finds an "element of truth" in it, because the "sphere of religion is the battlefield *par excellence* of the demonic."[18] He calls attention to the "horror and fear" with which the new converts on the mission fields have rejected the form of their old religion. Not even Christianity, as a historical phenomenon, can be exempt from the possibility of having evil influence:

> Religion, including the Christian religion, can be the sphere in which evil exhibits a power against which human reason and conscience are powerless. For religion is the sphere in which a man surrenders to something greater than himself. Even the strange idea that the similarities to Christianity in the non-Christian religions are evidences of demonic cunning points to an important truth. It is precisely at points of highest ethical and spiritual achievement that the religions find themselves threatened by, and therefore, arranged against the Gospel. It was the guardians of God's revelation who crucified the Son of God. It is the noblest among the Hindus who most emphatically reject

---

[17] *Open Secret*, 192.
[18] Ibid.

the Gospel. It is those who say, "we see," who seek to blot out the light (John 9:41).[19]

"Non-Christian Religions as Preparation for the Gospel"

This view sees religions as a preparation for Christ, and the Gospel fulfills them.[20] They are a "revelation of deep wants of the human spirit," which the Gospel satisfies. Newbigin sees this view as flawed because "such a view can be discussed only on the basis of an intimate and detailed knowledge of mankind's religions." Not all religions are asking the same question; each turns on its own different axis. Newbigin says,

> The questions Hinduism asks and answers are not the questions with which the Gospel is primarily concerned. One does not truly understand any of the religions by seeing it as a preparation for Christianity. Rather each religion must be understood on its own terms and along the line of its own central axis.[21]

Furthermore, some people view other religions as a source of many "values," but in Newbigin's opinion, the "values" of the religions do not together add up to him who alone is the truth.[22]

Roman Catholic Perspectives

In his survey of attitudes to other religions, Newbigin discusses two perspectives from the Roman Catholic Church.

Ecclesiam Suam (1964)

In this case,[23] the world religions are seen as forming concentric circles with the Roman Catholic Church at the centre and other Christians, Jews, Muslims, other theists, other religionists, and atheists placed

---

[19] Ibid., 193.
[20] This view is espoused by J. N. Farquhar, *The Crown of Hinduism* (Madras: Oxford University Press, 1915). It is fully expressed in the volume of the Edinburgh Conference of 1910 on the *Missionary Message* (New York: Revell, 1910), 247.
[21] *Open Secret*, 194.
[22] Ibid., 194.
[23] Ch. III, "The Dialogue."

progressively at greater distances. This way of looking at religions views them in terms of their distance from Christianity. According to Newbigin, this perspective "fails to do justice to the paradoxical fact that it is precisely those who are in one sense closest to the truth who are in another sense the bitterest opponents of the Gospel."[24] The other religions are not to be understood and measured by their proximity to or remoteness from Christianity. He asks, "Shall we say that the priest and the Levite, guardians of God's true revelation, are nearer to the center than the semipagan Samaritan?"[25]

Anonymous Christianity

Karl Rahner's conception of `Anonymous Christianity' views Christ as the only Saviour, but his saving work is extended beyond the bounds of the visible church. Newbigin places Rahner among the group of writers who, on the one hand, reject the exclusivism and, on the other hand, a total pluralism but contend that non-Christian religions are salvific.[26]

Rahner argues that Christianity is absolute religion, intended for all human beings, until the moment the Gospel really enters into the historical situation of an individual. Christianity does not simply confront the member of an extra-Christian religion as a mere non-Christian but as an anonymous Christian. In Rahner's thought, non-Christian religions are not on an equal level with the Church. He is developing his theses by taking into consideration the universal saving will of God and the elements of grace in non-Christian religions.[27]

Newbigin, however, does not believe that it is appropriate to call a Hindu or Muslim an "anonymous Christian" because doing so would be not to take his faith seriously.[28] Furthermore, this view holds that it is religion among all the activities of the human spirit that is the sphere of God's saving action, [29]which Newbigin rejects.

Two observations are in order here. First, Rahner, in his essay on "Christianity and the non-Christian Religions", does not seem to grapple

---

[24] *Open Secret*, 194 -195.
[25] Ibid., 195. See also *The Finality of Christ*, 44.
[26] Ibid. See also *Gospel*, 174 and *Open Secret*, 172. Rahner's view is found in his *Theological Investigations*, Vol. 5, 115 -134.
[27] "Christianity and Non-Christian Religions," *Theological Investigations*, Vol 5, 121. See Rahner's defense of the legitimacy of a non-Christian religion as a vehicle of salvation until it has been made explicit by the Gospel.
[28] *Open Secret*, 195.
[29] Ibid.

with the concept of 'religion' the way Newbigin does. Rahner's understanding of the word *religion* is not as limiting as Newbigin's. However, Newbigin fully agrees with Rahner on the manifestation of God's grace[30] and the spiritual fruits in the lives of the people of non-Christian religions, and yet he dismisses the possibility of anonymous Christianity. Although Newbigin acknowledges the "goodness that is found in every part of the human family," he says that there is a "dark side" to this bright picture. The "most dark and terrible thing" about the human nature is its capacity to take the good gifts of God and use them to "cut ourselves from God," to establish our independence from God.[31]

The insights of J. H. Bavinck are relevant here: these human religions may contain God's revelation, namely, the revelation of "God's hand and the result of human repression" or, in other words, the "divine approach and human rejection." Bavinck adds that "the great moments in the history of religion are the moments when God wrestled with man in a very particular way."[32] These religions may contain God's general revelation as well as the evidence of its rejection by the human heart.

Newbigin contends that religion is not the means of salvation,[33] but has unshakable faith in the absolute, adequate, and final revelation of God in Jesus Christ. This revelation is both unique and non-negotiable. It is Christocentric, and it serves as Newbigin's starting point in theology.[34] The death of Christ points to the "state of alienation, rejection and rebellion against him," which is an "unveiling of the infinite love of God" and the "unmasking of the dark horror of sin."[35] According to Newbigin, the reality of sin and the apostasy of the human heart can be dealt with only through the atoning death of Christ.

Those who speak of the salvific nature of non-Christian religions have not considered the "amazing grace of God" and the "appalling sin of the world." A "tension" exists between these two poles, and the temptation is to slacken the tension by drawing away from one or other of the two poles. Newbigin warns against the tendency to move toward some form

---

[30] *Gospel*, 175, where he states that within every human heart in the world there is the witness of God's grace.
[31] *Open Secret*, 199. The goodness found in humankind is due to its origin from the Creator, whose fatherhood everyone shares.
[32] Bavinck, 125.
[33] *Open Secret*, 200.
[34] Lesslie Newbigin, *Truth to Tell: The Gospel As Public Truth* (Grand Rapids: Eerdmans, 1991), 28. cf. *Gospel*, 175.
[35] *Gospel*, 175.

of universalism.[36] This tendency would blunt the issue that is raised by God's action in Christ for human souls. Those who write about the Gospel and the world's religions do not always seriously consider the fact of sin.[37]

According to Newbigin, Christianity is not the fulfillment of Hinduism. His question is: In what sense are the 'nobler' elements in the non-Christian religions becoming stepping-stones to Christian faith[38] Similarly, one cannot exclude the possibility that precisely religion may be the sphere of damnation - the place where the person is the farthest from the living God.[39] In light of the vast differences that exist among the religions of the world, it is difficult to generalize them.

Newbigin and Pluralist Theologians

The Gospel in a Pluralist Society is Newbigin's defense of Christian orthodoxy against religious pluralism, which has become a "contemporary orthodoxy" and the "reigning assumption" of the day. He engages a number of theologians, including Stanley Samartha, Paul Knitter, John Hick, Gordon Kaufman, and Wilfred Cantwell Smith, who consider the uniqueness of the Christian revelation as "myth."[40]

We will take just one example of a pluralist, namely, Stanley Samartha, whose support for a pluralist theology stems from several factors. *First*, the newly-formed post-colonial nations need to develop their own religio-cultural identity. *Second*, there are global environmental catastrophes and the possibility of nuclear death. *Third*, we need to stop the dangers of fascism and political ideology that would dominate people. *Fourth*, the need for alternative visions of life[41] is urgent. Samartha says that it is preposterous to assume that one religion alone has all the

---

[36] Ibid., 176.
[37] Ibid. Here he quotes the words of Anselm: *Nondum considerasti quanti ponderis sit peccatum.*
[38] *The Finality of Christ*, 26.
[39] Ibid., 43.
[40] John Hick and Paul Knitter, *The Myth of Christian Uniqueness* (Maryknoll, NY: Orbis Books, 1987), vii. This volume is particularly devoted to the reinterpretation of Christianity in mythological language. A number of theologians, including Newbigin, responded to this volume through D'Costa, Gavin, ed. *Christian Uniqueness Reconsidered: The Myth of a Pluralistic Theology of Religion* (Maryknoll, NY: Orbis Books, 1990).
[41] Ibid., 319.

resources to solve our global problems.⁴² Hence, we need pluralism to provide spiritual and cultural resources for the survival of people in their search for identity and dignity. He adds: "[P]lurality emphasizes that the Mystery of God or Truth or Dharma is too profound to be exhausted by any particular apprehensions of it." Because of the "immense dimensions" of global problems, we need the "availability of many resources to tackle these problems."⁴³

Newbigin agrees with the problems identified by Samartha, but the solution is not a radical reformulation of the Christian faith to deal with the new world situation. Samartha lacks faith in the adequacy of the Christian revelation in Jesus Christ alone. The idea of cooperation among all religions is to be supported, but this cooperation cannot be a substitute for the preaching of the Church. In his essay, Samartha uses the language of values, but these values cannot be separated from facts. Newbigin points out that Samartha "reveals his captivity to the post-Enlightenment worldview which separates facts from values and supposes that what are called values can be permanently sustained apart from some agreement about what are the facts."⁴⁴ The "values" of justice and compassion cannot be permanently sustained apart from some belief about the facts that correspond to these values. Take for example, the Orthodox Hindu belief about the miserable condition of the untouchable people in India. Their deplorable condition was believed to be the result of the sins of their previous birth, with which one cannot interfere. It was the preaching of the Gospel that brought about the change of view that has led to the making of legislation that would give them justice.⁴⁵

Newbigin upholds not only the validity and permanence of the once-for-all act of God's revelation in Christ but also rejects the very idea of individual subjectivity that emerges from the suggestions of pluralist theologies. Newbigin's point is that no one can consider every claim to divine revelation as equally valid. Moreover, it is not arrogance to affirm the unique decisiveness of God's action in Jesus Christ, because it is the greatest challenge to the arrogance of every culture to be itself the criterion by which others are judged.

In terms of the relation of Christianity to world religions, Newbigin is an exclusivist in the sense that he affirms the unique truth of the

---

[42] Stanley Samartha, "Looking Beyond Tambaram 1938," *International Review of Mission* LXXXVIII (1988): 315.
[43] Ibid., 319-20.
[44] *Gospel*, 158.
[45] Ibid.

revelation in Jesus Christ, but he is not exclusivist in the sense of denying the possibility of salvation of the non-Christian. He is inclusive in the sense that he refuses to limit the saving grace of God to the members of the Christian Church, but he rejects the inclusivism that teaches the concept of non-Christian religions being vehicles of salvation. He is pluralist in the sense of acknowledging the gracious work of God in the lives of all human beings, but he rejects a pluralism that denies the uniqueness and decisiveness of the act of God in Jesus Christ.[46]

Salvation of Non-Christians

Newbigin argues that the debate about the salvation of non-Christians has been "fatally flawed" because it has been conducted around the question, "Who can be saved?"[47] To put it plainly, the question is, "Where will one go when one dies?" In the debate about Christianity and the world's religions, there has been an almost unquestioned assumption that the only question is "What happens to the non-Christian after death?" In Newbigin's understanding, it is a wrong question. Why?

First, it is a question to which God alone has the right answer. Newbigin is "astounded at the arrogance of theologians" who think it is their duty to inform the world as to who is to be vindicated and who is to be condemned at the last judgment.[48] He criticizes Hans Küng, who is "scathing in contempt" for Protestant theologians who say that this question has to be left in the hands of God.[49] Newbigin says that we do not know in advance who is going to be saved and who is going to be lost. The judge on the last day is God and no one else. The day of judgment is a day of "surprises, reversals, and astonishment." In the parable of the sheep and the goats, both the saved and the lost are equally surprised. Therefore, one should see the tension in St. Paul between grace and sin, between the steadfast love of God and the need for a Christian to exercise severe self-discipline so as to be found in Christ (Romans 8; 1

---

[46] Ibid., 182-183. See also Harold Wells, *The Christic Center: Life-Giving and Liberating* (Maryknoll, NY: Orbis Books, 2004), 315, n.5.
[47] *Gospel*, 176.
[48] Ibid., 177.
[49] Reference is being made to Hans Küng's discussion of the Challenge of the World Religions in his *On Being a Christian*, trans. Edward Quinn (London: Collins, 1977), 99. Küng blames a number of theologians such as Barth, Bonhoeffer, Brunner, and Kraemer who are "without a closer knowledge and analysis of the real world of the religions."

Cor.9:27). The Christian life is lived in a magnetic field between the "amazing grace of God" and the "appalling sin of the world."[50]

The *second* objection to putting this question of salvation in this way is due to its nature of abstraction of the human soul from its real historical context. It is a reductionistic view, because the human person is not, essentially, a soul that can be understood in abstraction from the whole story of the person's life.[51] The question of salvation, therefore, should never be posed by abstracting it from God's history of salvation.[52]

Third, when the question is posed this way, it first of all deals with the individual's need for ultimate happiness, and not with God's glory. Christians must not "privatize" God's work of grace, seen from a selfish end. Thus, the 'glory of God', is more important than 'my salvation'.

So, what does Newbigin think of the salvation of the non-Christians? He would say, "I do not know." It is, as Gabriel Fackre has noted, an "intentional silence" maintaining "an eschatological agnosticism about the non-knowers of Jesus Christ."[53] By taking this position, is he not "failing to do his theological duty"? Here Newbigin's position is to be challenged the same way he challenged Hans Küng. Newbigin points out, "We cannot and must not try to know in advance what the final judgment is going to be."[54] To those who argue that a "good" Hindu will be saved, he asks about the criterion by which this goodness is measured. He wants to know how this goodness is related to the biblical emphasis upon the fact that Jesus came not for the righteous but for sinners.[55] He believes that God has appointed only the way of Christ, either to save or to provide unity for humanity. It is to this Christ-centered plan for which the Church has been made the firstfruit, sign, and instrument.[56]

---

[50] *Gospel*, 178.
[51] Ibid.
[52] Ibid., 178-179.
[53] Gabriel Fackre, "The Scandals of Particularity and Universality," *Mid-Stream* XXII (1983).
[54] "Christian Witness in a Plural Society," A paper presented to the Assembly of the British Council of Churches, London: British Council of Churches, 1977, 25.
[55] *The Finality of Christ*, 42.
[56] "Which Way for `Faith and Order'?" Reinhard Groscurth, ed., *What Unity Implies: Six Essays after Uppsala*, World Council Studies No. 7 (Geneva: WCC, 1969), 133.

Concluding Critical Comments

Throughout his engagement with non-Christian religions, Newbigin emphasizes the presence of divine grace in people of other religions. Christians must "expect, look for, and welcome" all the signs of divine grace in them. The Christian attitude that does not acknowledge their faith, the godliness, and the nobility is "deeply repulsive."[57] But the universal reality of sin and alienation point to the need for redemption through the work of Christ. They, too, are objects of God's salvation and, thus, are not excluded from the plan of redemption.

Also, Christians should cooperate with people of all faiths and ideologies in the projects of society, which are consistent with the Christian interpretation of history. The non-Christian understanding of the meaning and purpose of history may be different, but "along the way there will be many issues in which we can agree about what should be done."[58]

Finally, although we have shared commitments to the "business of the world" with people of other faiths, we shall discover the places where our ways must separate. In these commitments, others should come to know that our "context" and "goal" are different from theirs. Christians do not place their trust in the "intrahistorical goal" of their labors, but in the ultimate goal of history centered in Christ.[59] The participation of the Christians with the non-Christians in these societal projects creates occasions for telling them the Christian story of Jesus Christ.

---

[57] Ibid., 180.
[58] Ibid., 181.
[59] See Newbigin's affirmation of this point in his *Is Christ Divided?* (Grand Rapids: Eerdmans, 1961), 28.

BIBLIOGRAPHY

Bavinck, J.H. *The Church Between Temple and Mosque*, Grand Rapids: Eerdmans, 1967.
D'Costa, Gavin. ed., *Christian Uniqueness Reconsidered: The Myth of a Pluralistic Theology of Religion*, Maryknoll:: Orbis, 1990.
Eck, Diana. "The Religions and Tambaram: 1938 and 1988," *International Review of Mission*, Vol. LXXVII, 1988.
Fackre, Gabriel. "The Scandals of Particularity and Universality," *Mid-Stream*, Vol. XXII, 1, 1983.
Farquhar, J.N. *The Crown of Hinduism*. Madras: Oxford University Press, 1915.
Geertz, Clifford."Religion As a Cultural System," *The Interpretation of Cultures*. New York: Basic Books, 1973.
Hick, John & Paul Knitter. *The Myth of Christian Uniqueness*. Maryknoll, NY: Orbis Books, 1987.
Hick, John. *God and the Universe of Faiths*, London: The Macmillan Press, 1973.
Hunsberger, George. *The Missionary Significance of the Biblical Doctrine of Election As a Foundation for a Theology of Cultural Plurality in the Missiology of J.E.Lesslie Newbigin*, Ph.D. Dissertation, Princeton, New Jersey, 1987.
-----*Bearing the Witness of the Spirit: Lesslie Newbigin's Theology of Cultural Plurality*. Grand Rapids: Eerdmans, 1998.
Küng, Hans. *On Being a Christian*, trans. by Edwin Quinn, London: Collins, 1977.
Newbigin, Lesslie. *The Gospel in a Pluralist Society*, Grand Rapids: Eerdmans, 1989.
-----*The Finality of Christ*, London: SCM Press, 1969.
-----*Is Christ Divided?* Grand Rapids: Eerdmans, 1961.
-----*The Mission in Christ's Way*, Geneva: WCC Publications, 1987.
-----*The Open Secret: An Introduction to the Theology of Mission*, Grand Rapids, MI: Wm. B. Eerdmans Publishing Co., 1978.
-----*That All May Be One*, New York: Association Press, 1952.
-----*Truth to Tell: The Gospel as Public Truth*, Grand Rapids, MI: Wm. B. Eerdmans Publishing Co., 2001.
-----*Unfinished Agenda: An Autobiography*, Grand Rapids, MI: Wm. B. Eerdmans Publishing Co.,1985.
Otto, Rudolf. *India's Religion of Grace and Christianity Compared and Contrasted*, trans. By Foster, Frank Hugh, London: SCM Press, 1930.
Rahner, Karl. *Theological Investigations*, vol 5., trans. Karl-H. Kruger, London: Darton, Longman & Todd, 1966.
Samartha, Stanley. "Looking Beyond Tambaram 1938," *International Review of Mission*, Vol. LXXVII, 1988.
Smith, Wilfred Cantwell. "Mission, Dialogue, and God's Will for Us," *International Review of Mission*,Vol. LXXVII, 1988.
Thomas, J.M. *The Centrality of Christ and Inter-religious Dialogue in the Theology of Lesslie Newbigin*. Ph.D. Dissertation. Toronto: University of Toronto, 1996.

Wells, Harold G. *The Christic Center: Life-Giving and Liberating.* Maryknoll, NY: Orbis Books, 2004.

NOTES:

www.ingramcontent.com/pod-product-compliance
Lightning Source LLC
Chambersburg PA
CBHW071436160426
43195CB00013B/1918